Nature's

Thoreau on the Seasons

Nature's Panorama

THOREAU ON THE SEASONS

Edited by Ronald A. Bosco

Foreword by Robert D. Richardson Jr.

Engravings by Barry Moser

UNIVERSITY OF MASSACHUSETTS PRESS

AMHERST & BOSTON

Published in cooperation with

THE THOREAU SOCIETY

LC 2005005404
ISBN 1-55849-497-9 (library cloth ed.); 496-0 (paper)

Set in Monotype Bell
Printed on recycled paper by Thomson-Shore, Inc.

Library of Congress Cataloging-in-Publication Data

Thoreau, Henry David, 1817–1862.
Nature's panorama : Thoreau on the seasons / edited by Ronald A. Bosco ;
foreword by Robert D. Richardson, Jr.
p. cm. — (The spirit of Thoreau series)
Includes bibliographical references (p.   ).
ISBN 1-55849-496-0 (pbk. : alk. paper) —
ISBN 1-55849-497-9 (library cloth : alk. paper)
1. Thoreau, Henry David, 1817–1862—Quotations.
2. Seasons—Quotations, maxims, etc. 3. Nature—Quotations, maxims, etc.
I. Title: Thoreau on the seasons. II. Bosco, Ronald A. III. Title
IV. Series: Thoreau, Henry David, 1817–1862. Spirit of Thoreau.

PS3042.B68 2005
818'.309—dc22
2005005404

British Library Cataloguing in Publication data are available.

For Bernadette, Aaron, and Daryl—
Life's most wonderful companions in all seasons.

CONTENTS

FOREWORD

ROBERT D. RICHARDSON JR.

"WORKS AND DAYS were offered us," said Thoreau's friend Emerson, "and we took works." It was the wrong choice. He goes on to say "he only is rich who owns the day." This sounds easy, but is not, because the days, as he explains, "are of the least pretension and the greatest capacity of anything that exists." To say, as Emerson does, that the days are divine means that every day contains within it all the capacities of the universe, that every day is the day of creation and every day is the day of judgment. The trouble is, we don't always realize just how much we are being offered. Emerson wrote a poem about it, the central image of which haunted him all his life. "They [the days] come and go like muffled and veiled figures, sent from a distant friendly party; but they say nothing, and if we do not use the gifts they bring, they carry them as silently away."

Henry Thoreau not only understood this, he lived his life as though he actually believed it. Nothing else can account for his everyday ecstasy, his quotidian exaltation, his habitual elevation of the commonplace, his perpetual writing on the stretch. His prose is direct, imperative, optative, urgent. Watching snow-flakes one day he wrote, "a divinity must have stirred within them before the crystals did thus shoot and set. Wheels of the storm chariots. The same law that shapes the earth-star shapes the snow-star."

Thoreau paid attention to every single day and accepted as much from each as he could stagger home to his desk with. Thoreau noticed everything: how, when walking at night "the slightest inequalities in the ground are revealed by the shadows"; how in late August the pokeberry stems "are a deep rich purple . . . contrasting with clear green leaves"; how, in January, after an ice storm, "on the twigs of bushes for each bud there is a corresponding icy swelling." For every separate leaf or blade of grass he has ready, in John Ruskin's phrase, "a separate intention of the eye." Nothing is too small or too trivial for him. "I have," he once wrote, "the habit of attention to such excess that my senses get no rest, but suffer from a constant strain." Thoreau lived his whole life on sensory overload; his quenchless attention to each detail of every day brought him almost unmanageable riches. It has been said that Thoreau could get more out of ten minutes with a flower than most men could get out of a night with Cleopatra. "How to live—how to get the most life—how to extract its honey from the flower of the world. That," he wrote, "is my everyday business."

Every day. That is the key. "Nothing must be postponed," says Thoreau. "Take time by the forelock. Now or Never! You must live in the present, launch yourself on every wave, find your eternity in each moment." It is a question of attention. You are what you give your attention to. William James argued that the "whole drama of the voluntary life" hinges on the amount of attention we can bring to bear. James, like Thoreau, was fascinated by the role played by attention in our mental life; and James pushed it so far as to say that *"our belief and attention* are the same fact" (his italics). In other words, what we give our attention to *is* what we believe.

Thoreau was so conscious of this that he obliged every day to offer up some new belief. This is the reason his *Journal* is the great and always exciting masterpiece that it is. Walter Harding titled his fine biography *The Days of Henry Thoreau* to call attention to Thoreau's determination to live in each present day. And now the eminent scholar of Transcendentalism, Ronald A. Bosco, has produced the best compilation ever made from Thoreau's *Journal* by selecting passages each of which brings a ringing, brilliant-hued felt urgency to one day. Bosco has shaped the book as a chronicle of the New England seasons, a device Thoreau himself used to structure *Walden*. And those seasons are here, in all their glory, to be seen, heard, touched, tasted, and smelled by us. Now Thoreau calls our attention to a winter-sound, the "unrelenting steel cold scream of a jay, unmelted, that never flows into a song." Now he writes of June, "the month of grass and leaves. The deciduous trees are investing the evergreens and revealing how dark they are." Bosco has cleaned out the underbrush so Thoreau can take us on an excursion through the seasons of Concord, Massachusetts. "A year is made up," says Thoreau, "of a certain series and number of sensations and thoughts which have their language in nature. Now I am ice, now I am sorrel. Each experience reduces itself to a mood of the mind."

Thoreau begins with the four familiar seasons, those moods of the New England mind. But he knew that the Roman writer Varro had divided the year into six seasons, that the American Indians treated each moon as a season, and he may have known how the Chinese used to divide the year into twenty-four seasons. He certainly knew, from Linnaeus and from his own observation, that every day of the year brings some new bird or leaf or flower, some perceptible change to trees, and animals, and ponds. The project on which Thoreau was working when he died may have been designed to show how every single day is thus a new season with its own distinctive phenomena. At any event, Thoreau did understand that "the seasons and all their changes are in me." Emerson had insisted that the world exists for each one of us, and his advice was "build therefore your own world." Henry Thoreau took this imperative further than anyone else, and the result was his *Journal*. And what he has to say to us is: keep your *own* journal, find your *own* seasons, construct your *own* year, create your *own* calendar, and you will find, in the end, that you *have* built your own world.

INTRODUCTION
Thoreau's Romance of the Seasons
RONALD A. BOSCO

IDENTIFYING a parallel between those autumnal signs always evident to a New Englander that the year is coming to an end and his sense of the frailty of human life, on the evening of 1 November 1858 Henry David Thoreau opened his journal and engaged in an extended meditation on the relation between the seasons and himself. His meditation was well timed, for the first of November inaugurated what Thoreau had more than once characterized as "November Eat-heart," a season that, with its increasingly dark days and lifeless prospect, chilled the poetic impulse and almost "oblige[d] a man to eat his own heart" in order to know that he was alive (25 November 1857; 13 November 1851, *Journal* 4:180). Earlier on this particular day Thoreau had walked through Sleepy Hollow, up to Poplar Hill, and along the banks of the Concord River, and as he did so, he noticed the prospect before him becoming progressively grim, if not actually gothic. The trees were bare, their leaves having already put on that spectacular show of color associated with New England autumns and fallen to the ground. Their prime a distant memory, flowers and fruits—those that grew wild, and those that were tended under the farmer's watchful eye—had all gone to seed in Concord's meadows and fields, creating a bleakness in the landscape which could only remind the observer that the twilight of the year had arrived and deliver him an unwelcome sign of his own mortality. In place of summer's enchanting rhythms—the melodies of birds, the croaking of frogs, the splashing of fish in ponds and streams—silence had descended on the world, and too quickly, it seemed, the afternoons had grown shorter, compounding silence with darkness. Hardly a cricket was to be heard as banks of ominous clouds gathered soundlessly across the horizon, foretelling the onset of winter and divining the secret ennui of those who, in turning indoors at this season for protection from the elements, may have also shut themselves away from opportunities to experience life and love.

For a person of lesser natural wisdom and imagination than Thoreau possessed, this scene could easily have been devastating. *Ennui,* which is Thoreau's word, aptly describes the feeling that stirs in the observer whose mind and sensibility are narrowly concentrated on the stark and bleak character of the landscape at this moment. With no recognition of what we may call "the larger picture"—a recognition that the moment is a completely natural and transitory one, one that has been carefully prepared for by the year's winter, spring, summer, and early autumn, one that is a necessary prelude to new winters, new springs, new summers, and new autumns—such an observer of this scene can only regard it as nature's last twilight and the harbinger of his own death. But on this day Thoreau found it otherwise. For him, this was a moment full of lyric possibility, so much so that he wondered, "What new sweet was I to extract from it?" Neither nature's nor his own last twilight, this moment warmed him "as a familiar thing come round again," as a frame in a moving picture or, as he referred to it in both the technical and the literary senses, as a part of "a panorama . . . with which [he] was perfectly familiar just coming into view." For Thoreau, this moment was yet another cheering frame in nature's rolling panorama of the seasons, a moment in her "infinitely sweet and grand" cycle of birth, maturation, seeding, death, and regeneration, and as a spectator of and participant in that cycle, he was "prepared to be pleased."

And he was indeed pleased. As Thoreau shares with us the lesson he has drawn from his meditation on this day, we learn that "with perfect contentment" he embraced this new November as an old friend who had been away too long, and that he was unwilling to exchange this or any other November "vision . . . for any treasure or heaven that could be imagined." Transforming "November twilights" into "indispensable starlight," he portrays the return of November each year as a salutary instance of the constancy with which nature preserves the seasons in their "orbit" and with which, while guaranteeing new life for the landscape the following year, nature also guarantees growth and new life in Thoreau himself. What he and others have labeled "November Eat-heart," Thoreau now identifies as a season of "infinite expectation and faith." After considering "the difference between me and myself a year ago," he admits to being encouraged by the onset of this new November, and as he carefully gathers to mind each sign of the season as his intellectual and imaginative "fuel for the approaching winter," he looks forward to that season as a time to enjoy his "ever new self" in winter tramps in new-fallen snow, skating expeditions across frozen ponds and meadows, and renewed associations with winter birds.

By the time he identified November 1858 as ushering in a season of "infinite expectation and faith," Thoreau, who was born in Concord in 1817 and died there in 1862, had already lived the greater part of his career as a literary naturalist, philosopher, and saunterer in Concord's woods and fields. The major events and writings that we associate with him today were literally behind him. Between 1845 and 1847, he had sojourned at Walden Pond, and in *Walden* (1854), that masterpiece of American prose, Thoreau re-created his experience, using it also as a means to enlarge on what he believed were the opportunities and the limitations for self-culture inherent in America. In *A Week on the Concord and Merrimack Rivers* (1849), Thoreau recounted a trip he had taken in 1839 with his brother, John, on those rivers, and in doing so he not only paid tribute to a then-deceased brother whom he dearly loved, but also announced himself as an enthusiastic—though patient and meticulous—observer of the New England landscape and an early prophet of American literary environmentalism. Between 1838 and 1857 he traveled three times to the Maine woods, and between 1849 and 1857 he visited Cape Cod on four occasions. In his expansive journal, which he began in 1837 at the suggestion of his mentor and friend Ralph Waldo Emerson and continued until the end of 1861 when deteriorating health prevented him from making additional entries, Thoreau recorded all that he saw and felt in the Maine woods and on Cape Cod. Although he did not live long enough to bring the literary finish necessary for publication to either set of journeys, the spontaneity, originality, and depth of his observations and reflections while on them are preserved in many of the fourteen volumes of his *Journal* and in *The Maine Woods* (1864) and *Cape Cod* (1865), two posthumous works edited by Thoreau's sister Sophia and his friend Ellery Channing.

So why, one might wonder, was Thoreau so moved to meditate at length on the November spectacle he witnessed in 1858? What convictions did the walk he took on that particular November day awaken in him? What underlying literary impulse or philosophical bias encouraged him to rewrite the depressing facts so obvious in the landscape into a hymn of praise for this moment in nature's panorama and proclaim, at the end of his journal entry, "Here I am at home"?

There is only one answer to these questions. Thoreau's response to this particular day was not a reiteration of what his published and private writings already revealed about his reverence for the seasons and nature's constancy in providing them for the encouragement, illumination, and consolation of humankind; it was, rather, his response to a day lived according to a lifelong rule that also serves us as a measure of his character. "There is no world for the penitent and regretful," Thoreau once remarked, meaning thereby that one had to be always at the ready to leap into nature and never look back. "Nothing must be postponed." To know oneself, one had to be open to all seasonal influences, "not . . . governed by rigid rules, as by the almanac," but governed by those influences that spontaneously disclosed the secrets of nature's meandering days and revealed meanings that lay otherwise hidden in the recesses of the individual's feelings and thoughts. "The moods and thoughts of man," Thoreau believed, "are revolving just as steadily and incessantly as nature's," and he believed further that those moods and thoughts—both man's and nature's—revolved and evolved in concert with each other (24 April 1859).

Thus, Thoreau woke to every day filled with "infinite expectation and faith" and always "prepared to be pleased." Every day he woke not only to a world that was new to his eye, but also to a world in which nature was still fully engaged in the divine act of creation (20 January 1855). Every day offered him a fresh opportunity to take delight in nature's panorama for its own sake, to identify and cultivate his "ever new self" in the ever new cycles of the seasons, and to use imagination to "navigate" his way through daily walks and transform the variable prospects before him into meditations on nature's secret but retrievable lessons (6 November 1853). Confident that nature possessed "pristine vigor" sufficient to sustain any human heart

(6 January 1858), daily Thoreau set out to allow nature to "unfold" previously hidden correspondences between the alternating cycles of the seasons and those of his own thoughts and moods, and so to find himself, in reflections made during and after his walks, redeemed from the care of temporary climatic or personal changes and "in harmony with the longer periods of nature" (7 January 1842).

Thoreau found his walks in nature both "sanative" and "poetic." Alone in spring- or summertime sun-drenched meadows or "in distant woods or fields . . . even [on] a bleak and . . . cheerless day," he respected all objects as "elevating" and prized their capacity to inspire "serene and profitable thought" in him. Regardless of the season, Thoreau felt that he was always "at home" in nature and "grandly related" to thoughts and moods larger than his own. In nature, where, as Emerson expressed it, all mean egotism vanished (*Nature, CW*, 1:10), Thoreau met up with his "serene, immortal, infinitely encouraging . . . companion" and saw "out and around [him]self." Stepping outside of himself in walks across the seasons of nature, Thoreau reported, "I come to myself." Exulting in a typical mood of optimism reinforced by his observation of the constancy of nature, he expressed confidence that through his sympathy with the seasons "the problem of existence [was] simplified," and that with the problem of his existence simplified, he could meet the ethical challenge to which he daily turned to nature for instruction: "I wish to be made better" (7 January 1857).

Two years before his death Thoreau wrote, "A man receives only what he is ready to receive, whether physically or intellectually or morally, as animals conceive at certain seasons . . . only" (5 January 1860). Not surprisingly, perhaps, given his receptiveness to nature's seasonal lessons, Thoreau's earliest known written work is "The Seasons" (1828 or 1829). Composed in his first year at the Concord Academy as he was approaching his teenage years, this brief essay shows Thoreau sensitive to the pastoral tradition in nature writing in which the observer's ability to capture the seasonal beauty, colors, and sounds of the landscape and to express them through emotive language serves as an index to his sympathy with nature and openness to the larger forces that move through and guide her. This essay also shows Thoreau preoccupied with the seasonal clock that literally kept the time of everyday life in rural nineteenth-century America:

> Why do the Seasons change? and why
> Does Winter's stormy brow appear?
> It is the word of him on high,
> Who rules the changing varied year.

There are four Seasons in a year, Spring, Summer, Autumn, and Winter. I will begin with Spring. Now we see the ice beginning to thaw, and the trees to bud. Now the Winter wears away, and the ground begins to look green with the new born grass. The birds which have lately been to more southern countries return again to cheer us with their morning song.

Next comes Summer. Now we see a beautiful sight. The trees and flowers are in bloom.— Now is the pleasantest part of the year. Now the fruit begins to form . . . and all things look beautiful.

In Autumn we see the trees loaded with fruit. Now the farmers begin to lay in their Winter's store. . . . The trees are partly stripped of their leaves. The birds . . . are now retiring to warmer countries, as they know Winter is coming.

> Next comes Winter. Now we see the ground covered with snow, and the trees are bare. The cold is so intense that the rivers and brooks are frozen.— There is nothing green to be seen. We have no birds to cheer us with their morning song. We hear only the sound of the sleigh bells. (*Early Essays and Miscellanies*, 3)

Except for his increasingly mature command of prose and more daring incursions into nature, in "The Seasons" Thoreau established the basic terms of his lifelong devotion to nature and openness to all of her seasonal influences as means to sustain the life of his intellect and imagination and sound the depth of his own humanity. Believing that "[t]he boundaries of the actual are no more fixed & rigid—than the elasticity of our imaginations" (31 May 1853), Thoreau denied himself no experience, no matter how trivial or extravagant it might have appeared to others, as long as he could enjoy it in nature. He thought it a "luxury" reserved just for him "to stand up to [his] chin in some retired swamp for a whole summer's day, scenting the sweet fern and bilberry blows," "lulled by the minstrelsy of gnats and mosquitoes," and cheered by "genial and familiar converse with the leopard frog" (16 June 1840). He thought it equally luxurious to be out in a snowstorm, watch as transparent "beautiful star crystals" lodged on his coat, and reflect on the fact that, just as "these glorious spangles, the sweeping of heaven's floor," fell on him and brightened his immediate surroundings, so too they fell on and brightened "the restless squirrel's fur, . . . the far-stretching fields and forests, the wooded dells, and the mountain-tops." In the winter snow, as in the summer swamp, Thoreau felt himself expand to an existence as wide as the universe, and he received yet another confirmation of his chief article of faith: "Nature is full of genius, full of divinity" (5 January 1856).

Thoreau's Concord world, which he considered as fair "as the valhalla of the gods," was, he believed, designed to answer his every question, satisfy his every yearning, and fulfill his every dream. Opening himself to all natural influences in the rural landscape around him, a landscape in which he felt himself "God-propt" "whole and entire," he thought himself rewarded with a world "gilded" for his delight, a place where, he wrote, "holidays are prepared for me—& my path is strewn with flowers" (15 December 1841; 17 August 1851). Immersed in that world, Thoreau defined his "profession" as "to be always on the alert to find God in nature—to know his lurking places. To attend all the oratorios—the operas in nature" (7 September 1851). Following that profession, he renewed his long-neglected kinship with lichens; believed that as he sailed on the river, he was "blown on by God's breath" and could feel both the sail of his boat and the sail of his soul "fill gently out with the breeze"; improved upon his label for wild apples—"'To be eaten in the wind'"—to discriminate between thoughts for the field and those for the house; felt the aspens' trembling in a June breeze induce "a little [flutter] in [his] thoughts"; found himself immediately "thinking, philosophizing, moralizing" on hearing the "first cricket['s] chirrup" in the spring; imaginatively embraced a "shrub oak with its scanty garment of leaves rising above the snow" and fell in love with her; and finally declared all nature to be his bride (15 December 1841; 30 June 1840; 27 October 1855; 6 June 1857; 15 May 1853; 1 December 1856; 23 April 1857, respectively). From the beginning to the very end of his career, Thoreau devoted himself to "homely every-day phenomena and adventures," relishing every opportunity to rejoice in those sympathies that he discovered he shared with nature, guarding the richness of a rustic life which permitted him to "[t]hrow away a whole day for a single expansion[,] a single inspiration of air" (21 August 1851), and daily marveling at, as he wrote, "my surprise that I should have been born into the most estimable place in all the world, and in the very nick of time, too" (5 December 1856).

In confessing his good fortune at having been born in just the right place "in the very nick of time," Thoreau paid tribute not only to Concord as his muse and the site in which he fashioned his life as a unique expression of radical individualism, but also to two major contemporary influences that provided him with the literary and philosophic license to shape himself in nature's image. Our recognition of those influences hardly lessens the originality or authority of Thoreau's work and thought; rather, our recognition of them justifies the belief long held by many of his followers that Henry Thoreau's life represents the most complete expression of the possibilities for self-culture in nineteenth-century America. Those influences are the British Romantic tradition—which is probably most apparent in the poetry of William Wordsworth, Percy Bysshe Shelley, and John Keats—and American Transcendental philosophy as Emerson announced it in *Nature* in 1836.

In brief, the literary and philosophic license that Thoreau received from the British Romantics conferred legitimacy on his preoccupation with the aesthetics and ethics of the commonplace—with, as he wrote, the beauty and moral instruction inherent in "homely every-day phenomena and adventures." Romantic theory and practice encouraged Thoreau's reliance on intuition and feeling as sources of new knowledge superseding that arrived at through either reason or the revelations of outworn religious creeds, and his reliance, as well, on meditation and memory as means to fathom and improve upon the meaning of feelings after their initial experience. In their poems the Romantics developed a number of themes that derived from their wonder at nature's prospect and their musings on human-kind's relation to nature; those themes, which are evident in the prose poetry of Thoreau's books and journal, include the iden-tification of God with nature; belief in the superiority of rustic to civilized or conventional life, with nature providing one with an inexhaustible source of inspiration and physical and mental health; confidence that one's closeness to nature could amelio-rate the dark side of human nature; and confidence, too, that a life led in concert with nature's seasonal cycles was a sure prelude to immortality.

Less a matter of contrast than an adaptation of the British Romantics' vision to the American landscape and the demo-cratic impulse that was hardly exhausted in the Revolution that had occurred a generation before Thoreau's birth, Tran-scendentalism was grounded in the belief that God is immanent in all aspects of the creation. "Revelation," Emerson preached in the same year that *Nature* appeared, "is not closed and sealed[;] . . . the Creation is an endless miracle as new at this hour as when Adam awoke in the garden" (*CS*, 4:246). Emerson's *Nature* was a sweeping declaration of the divinity of human life and the universality of thought. Drawing from Platonic and Eastern thought, natural history, and the British Romantic tra-dition, Emerson proclaimed nature the resource through which individuals could restore "original and eternal beauty" to their universe and achieve the redemption of their souls (*Nature, CW*, 1:43). In its appeal to intuition and the senses, its con-viction that language, like any other material fact, is symbolic of a higher spiritual reality that governs the universe, and its song of the "Orphic poet"—reminding modern man that he is descended from a figure who before time began "was permeated and dissolved by spirit" and "filled nature with his overflowing currents" (*Nature, CW,* 1:42)—Emersonian Transcendentalism proposed a new gospel, which Emerson later defined as "the infinitude of the private man" (*JMN,* 7:342), and it provided the generation into which Thoreau was born with one commandment: "'Build . . . your own world'" (*Nature, CW,* 1:45). Because it relied entirely on intuition and regarded the universe as both dressed up in symbols and a symbol itself, the philosophy that Thoreau and others of his generation inherited from Transcendentalism was not a systematic philosophy in the strict sense; it was rather, as Thoreau wrote, an analogical philosophy that validated the subjective experience of every life as means to transform human deserts into poetic paradises (6 May 1854).

In virtually all of his journal writings on the seasons which follow in this volume, Thoreau betrays his debt to both British Romantic and American Transcendentalist influences. What is crucial to notice while reading these selections, however, is not their evidence of Thoreau's debt to such influences, but his unique appropriation and transformation of them to his own distinctive purpose.

For instance, in the opening selection, when Thoreau identifies nature's constancy in the return of the seasons as a prediction of his own immortality, echoes of Wordsworth's "Ode: Intimations of Immortality from Recollections of Early Childhood" seem to resonate, and especially so as Thoreau recognizes "this steady persistency and recovery of Nature as a quality of myself" and decides that "[t]he eternity which I detect in Nature I predicate of myself" (23 March 1856). Similarly, Wordsworth's encomium on the virtues of childhood in the "Ode" and Emerson's homiletic confidence in the continuation of the miracle of creation seem to inform Thoreau's thoughts when he writes on another occasion: "My imagination, my love & reverence & admiration, my sense of the miraculous is not so excited by any event as by the remembrance of my youth. Men talk about bible miracles because there is no miracle in their lives" (9 June 1850).

Yet these selections are neither Wordsworthian in the first instance nor a variation on Wordsworthian and Emersonian impulses in the second: They are entirely Thoreauvian. While in the first instance Thoreau consoles himself by noticing his share in the constancy of nature, his real purpose in this passage is to indict those who have disrupted the flow of nature's redemptive power and, literally, taken the poetry out of the American environment. The professional naturalist who understood his mission "to be always on the alert to find God in nature— . . . [to] attend all . . . the operas in nature," here finds himself listening "to a concert in which so many parts are wanting." The aspect of nature that interests him most—"Primitive Nature"—is gone. Taking pains "to know all the phenomena of spring"—including the great animal migrations by which native tribes once marked the season—Thoreau is distressed to find that the nature he possesses is an "imperfect copy" of the original "poem," his ancestors having "torn out many of the first leaves and grandest passages, and mutilated it in many places," and left him only an "emasculated" landscape that he must restore to life through his imagination.

Thoreau's judgment is even more dramatically apparent in the second passage, when, after acknowledging that remembrance of his youth awakens his "sense of the miraculous" though the "miracle" seems to have gone out of most men's lives, he says, "Cease to gnaw that crust." The ambiguity of Thoreau's intention in that command—Is it a command directed at himself to stop living in the past? Is it a critique of the values of those fellow men who have lost their sense of the miraculous?—suggests that he is writing well beyond Emerson's frame of reference, which is most often "the world I *think*" ("Experience," *CW,* 3:48). Thoreau's world is not one constructed out of self-indulgent thought, but one constructed out of actual hard work in which the ideal laborer, whether he be an artist, a shopworker, or a naturalist, achieves self-culture by maintaining single-minded devotion to his profession. Thoreau's laborer always looks forward, assured by "patient and unanxious labor at the anvil that fairer mornings are to be compelled" (5 October 1840), and so he never gnaws at the "crust" of his past or of regret. His is work that reminds Thoreau of the annual plowing and planting that are seasonal realities, not abstract thoughts, for the farmer. The farmer's work is "work that tells, that concerns all men, which the sun shines and the rain falls on, and the birds sing over"; it is work that, like Thoreau's, "comes pretty near to making a world" (28 March 1857).

In a passage that he entered in his journal in 1853, Thoreau succinctly expressed the core of his philosophy, described the fundamental character of his life as an analogical naturalist, and explained how he revered each waking day as a moment of "infinite expectation and faith"; in doing so, he also justified his lifelong romance with the seasons:

> He is richest who has most use for nature as raw material of tropes and symbols with which to describe his life. If these gates of golden willows affect me, they correspond to the beauty and promise of some experience on which I am entering. If I am overflowing with life, am rich in experience for which I lack expression, then nature will be my language full of poetry,—all

nature will *fable*, and every natural phenomenon be a myth. The man of science, who is not seeking for expression but for a fact to be expressed merely, studies nature as a dead language. I pray for such inward experience as will make nature significant. (10 May 1853, *Journal* V:135)

The Concord landscape over which Thoreau sauntered for almost his entire life served him an inexhaustible array of tropes and symbols through which to describe, understand, and complete his life. Those tropes and symbols he discerned in Concord's "regular phenomena of the seasons" were "at last . . . [as] they were *at first*, . . . simply and plainly phenomena or phases of [his] life" (26 October 1857). Thus, just as the features of that landscape were constantly altered by seasonal rhymes that nature never "tire[d] of repeating," so Thoreau never wearied of repeatedly translating the "solid beauty" of the changing landscape into a near-infinite variety of fables of himself that he could "navigate" and comprehend through imagination. Capturing the poetry of nature's seasonal panorama and translating it into passages of his life, in his journal Thoreau transformed his life into "an epic in blank verse, enriched with a million tinkling rhymes" (7 December 1856). Sometimes in the journal passages that follow readers will find Thoreau reporting those rhymes as fanciful suggestions he has projected into nature's poem, as when he imagines that cobwebs stretched across a dewy lawn are "gossamer veils . . . dropped from the fairy shoulders that danced on the grass the past night" (7 July 1852), or when he believes that sunset colors resting on andromeda leaves transfigure these "rubies of the swamp" into "a hundred ruby throated humming birds" (23 May 1853). But always in the passages that follow readers will find Thoreau living in

Introduction

each season of nature's panorama as it passes, breathing the air, drinking the drink, tasting the fruit, and resigning himself to the influences of each (23 August 1853). Immersed in nature and enlarged by her rolling panorama of the seasons, Thoreau navigated Concord's landscape as a "faery-place" where, as he and nature collaborated in constructions of his "ever new self," he confirmed "the immortality of [his] soul" (9 October 1851).

NATURE'S PANORAMA
Thoreau on the Seasons

SPRING

I SPEND a considerable portion of my time observing the habits of the wild animals, my brute neighbors. By their various movements and migrations they fetch the year about to me. Very significant are the flight of geese and the migration of suckers. . . . But when I consider that the nobler animals have been exterminated here,—the cougar, panther, lynx, wolverine, wolf, bear, moose, deer, the beaver, the turkey, etc., etc.,—I cannot but feel as if I lived in a tamed, and, as it were, emasculated country. Would not the motions of those larger and wilder animals have been more significant still? Is it not a maimed and imperfect nature that I am conversant with? As if I were to study a tribe of Indians that had lost all its warriors. Do not the forest and the meadow now lack expression, now that I never see nor think of the moose with a lesser forest on his head in the one, nor of the beaver in the other? When I think what were the various sounds and notes, the migrations and works, and changes of fur and plumage which ushered in the spring and marked the other seasons of the year, I am reminded that this my life in nature, this particular round of natural phenomena which I call a year, is lamentably incomplete. I listen to [a] concert in which so many parts are wanting. The whole civilized country is to some extent turned into a city, and I am that citizen whom I pity. Many of those animal migrations and other phenomena by which the Indians marked the season are no longer to be observed. I seek acquaintance with Nature,—to know her moods and manners. Primitive Nature is the most interesting to me. I take pains to know all the phenomena of the spring, for instance, thinking that I have here the entire poem, and then, to my chagrin, I hear that it is but an imperfect copy that I possess and have read, that my ancestors have torn out many of the first leaves and grandest passages, and mutilated it in many places. I should not like to think that some demigod had come before me and picked out some of the best of the stars. I wish to know an entire heaven and an entire earth. All the great trees and beasts, fishes and fowl are gone. The streams, perchance, are somewhat shrunk. . . .

I think I may say that the snow has been *not less than a foot deep on a level* in open land until to-day. . . . The bare ground begins to appear where the snow is worn in the street. It has been steadily melting since March 13th. . . .

The east side of the Deep Cut is nearly bare, as is the railroad itself, and, on the driest parts of the sandy slope, I go looking for *Cicindela,*—to see it run or fly amid the sere blackberry vines,—some life which the warmth of the dry sand under the spring sun has called forth. . . . I am reassured and reminded that I am the heir of eternal inheritances which are inalienable, when I feel the warmth reflected from this sunny bank, and see the yellow sand and the reddish subsoil, and hear some dried leaves rustle and the trickling of melting snow in some sluiceway. The eternity which I detect in Nature I predicate of myself also. How many springs I have had this same experience! I am encouraged, for I recognize this steady persistency and recovery of Nature as a quality of myself.

23 March 1856, Journal *VIII:220–23*

Spring

❧ WALK TO CARDINAL SHORE and sail to Well Meadow and Lee's Cliff. . . .

We cross to Lee's shore and sit upon the bare rocky ridge overlooking the flood southwest and northeast. It is quite sunny and sufficiently warm. I see one or two of the small fuzzy gnats in the air. The prospect thence is a fine one, especially at this season, when the water is high. The landscape is very agreeably diversified with hill and vale and meadow and cliff. As we look southwest, how attractive the shores of russet capes and peninsulas laved by the flood! Indeed, that large tract east of the bridge is now an island. How fair that low, undulating russet land! At this season and under these circumstances, the sun just come out and the flood high around it, russet, so reflecting the light of the sun, appears to me the most agreeable of colors, and I begin to dream of a russet fairyland and elysium. How dark and terrene must be green! but this smooth russet surface reflects almost all the light. That broad and low but firm island, with but few trees to conceal the contour of the ground and its outline, with its fine russet sward, firm and soft as velvet, reflecting so much light,—all the undulations of the earth, its nerves and muscles, revealed by the light and shade, and even the sharper ridgy edge of steep banks where the plow has heaped up the earth from year to year,—this is a sort of fairyland and elysium to my eye. The tawny couchant island! Dry land for the Indian's wigwam in the spring, and still strewn with his arrow-points. The sight of such land reminds me of the pleasant spring days in which I have walked over such tracts, looking for these relics. How well, too, this smooth, firm, light-reflecting, tawny earth contrasts with the darker water which surrounds it,—or perchance lighter sometimes! At this season, when the russet colors prevail, the contrast of water and land is more agreeable to behold. What an inexpressibly soft curving line is the shore! Or if the water is perfectly smooth and yet rising, you seem to see it raised an eighth of an inch with swelling lip above the immediate shore it kisses, as in a cup or . . . a saucer. Indian isles and promontories. Thus we sit on that rock, hear the first wood frog's croak, and dream of a russet elysium. Enough for the season is the beauty thereof. Spring has a beauty of its own which we would not exchange for that of summer, and at this moment, if I imagine the fairest earth I can, it is still russet, such is the color of its blessed isles, and they are surrounded with the phenomena of spring.

23 March 1859, Journal *XII:71, 74–76*

❧ WHEN I WITNESS the first plowing and planting, I acquire a long-lost confidence in the earth,—that it will nourish the seed that is committed to its bosom. I am surprised to be reminded that there is warmth in it. We have not only warmer skies, then, but a warmer earth. The frost is out of it, and we may safely commit these seeds to it. . . . Yesterday I walked with Farmer beside his team and saw one furrow turned quite round in his field. What noble work is plowing, with the broad and solid earth for material, the ox for fellow-laborer, and the simple but efficient plow for tool! Work that is not done in any shop, in a cramped position, work that tells, that concerns all men, which the sun shines and the rain falls on, and the birds sing over! You turn over the whole vegetable mould, expose how many grubs, and put a new aspect on the face of the earth. It comes pretty near to making a world.

28 March 1857, Journal *IX:310–11*

Spring

❦ How CHARMING the contrast of land and water, especially a
temporary island in the flood, with its new and tender shores
of waving outline, so withdrawn yet habitable, above all if it
rises into a hill high above the water and contrasting with it
the more, and if that hill is wooded, suggesting wildness! Our
vernal lakes have a beauty to my mind which they would not
possess if they were more permanent. Everything is in rapid
flux here, suggesting that Nature is alive to her extremities
and superficies. To-day we sail swiftly on dark rolling waves
or paddle over a sea as smooth as a mirror, unable to touch
the bottom, where mowers work and hide their jugs in August;
coasting the edge of maple swamps, where alder tassels and
white maple flowers are kissing the tide that has risen to meet
them. But this particular phase of beauty is fleeting. Nature has
so many shows for us she cannot afford to give much time to
this. In a few days, perchance, these lakes will all run away
to the sea. Such are the pictures she paints. When we look at
our masterpieces we see only dead paint and its vehicle, which
suggests no liquid life rapidly flowing off from beneath. In the
former case—in Nature—it is constant surprise and novelty. In
many arrangements there is a wearisome monotony. We know
too well what [we] shall have for our Sunday's dinner, but each
day's feast in Nature's year is a surprise to us and adapted to our
appetite and spirits. She has arranged such an order of feasts as
never tires. Her motive is not economy but satisfaction.

As we sweep past the north end of Poplar Hill, with a sand-
hole in it, its now dryish, pale-brown mottled sward clothing
its rounded slope, which was lately saturated with moisture,
presents very agreeable hues. In this light, in fair weather, the
patches of now dull-greenish mosses contrast just regularly
enough with the pale-brown grass. It is like some rich but

modest-colored Kidderminster carpet, or rather the skin of a monster python tacked to the hillside and stuffed with earth. These earth colors, methinks, are never so fair as in the spring. Now the green mosses and lichens contrast with the brown grass, but ere long the surface will be uniformly green. I suspect that we are more amused by the effects of color in the skin of the earth now than in summer. Like the skin of a python, greenish and brown, a coat for it to creep over the earth and be concealed in. Or like the skin of a pard, the great leopard mother that Nature is, where she lies at length, exposing here flanks to the sun. I feel as if I could land to stroke and kiss the very sward, it is so fair. . . . Such ottomans and divans are spread for us to recline on. Nor are these colors mere thin superficial figures, vehicles for paint, but wonderful living growths,—these lichens to the study of which learned men have devoted their lives,—and libraries have been written about them. The earth lies out now like a leopard, drying her lichen and moss spotted skin in the sun, her sleek and variegated hide. I know that the few raw spots will heal over. Brown is the color for me, the color of our coats and out daily lives, the color of the poor man's loaf. The bright tints are pies and cakes, good only for October feasts, which would make us sick if eaten every day.

28 March 1859, Journal *XII:95–98*

🌱 6 AM. To the river side & Merrick's Pasture. The sun is up. The water on the meadows is perfectly smooth & placid reflecting the hills & clouds & trees. The air is full of the notes of birds—song sparrows—red-wings—robins (singing a strain) blue birds—& I hear also a lark— As if all the earth had burst forth into song. The influence of this April morning

Spring

has reached them for they live out of doors . . . and there is no danger that they will oversleep themselves such a morning. A few weeks ago before the birds had come [there] came to my mind in the night the twittering sound of birds in the early dawn of a spring morning—a semi prophecy of it—and last night I attended mentally as if I heard the spray-like dreaming sound of the mid summer frog—& realized how glorious & full of revelations it was. Expectation may amount to prophecy.

2 April 1852, Journal *4:415*

❦ THE BAY-WING NOW SINGS—the first I have been able to hear— . . . singing loud and clear and incessantly. It sings with a pleasing deliberation, contrasting with the spring vivacity of the song sparrow, whose song many would confound it with. It comes to revive with its song the dry uplands and pastures and grass-fields about the skirts of villages. Only think how finely our life is furnished in all its details,—sweet wild birds provided to fill its interstices with song! It is provided that while we are employed in our corporeal, or intellectual, or other, exercises we shall be lulled and amused or cheered by the singing of birds. When the laborer rests on his spade to-day, the sun having just come out, he is not left wholly to the mercy of his thoughts, nature is not a mere void to him, but he can hardly fail to hear the pleasing and encouraging notes of some newly arrived bird. The strain of the grass finch is very likely to fall on his ear and convince him, whether he is conscious of it or not, that the world is beautiful and life a fair enterprise to engage in. It will make him calm and contented. If you yield for a moment to the impressions of sense, you hear some bird giving expression to its happiness in a pleasant strain. We are provided with singing birds and with ears to hear them. What an institution that! Nor are we obliged to catch and cage them, nor to be bird-fanciers in the common sense. Whether a man's work be hard or easy, whether he be happy or unhappy, a bird is appointed to sing to a man while he is at his work.

15 April 1859, Journal *XII:143–44*

❦ IT IS A VIOLENT N E STORM in which it is very difficult & almost useless to carry an umbrella. . . . The meadows are higher—more wild & angry & the waves run higher with more white to their caps than before this year. I expect to hear of ship wrecks—& of . . . damage done by the tide. This wind too keeps the water in the river. It is worth the while to walk today to hear the rumbling roar of the wind—as if it echoed through the hollow chambers of the air. It even sounds like thunder sometimes— . . . The wind sounds even in open fields as if on a roof over our heads. . . . What comes flapping low with heavy wing over the middle of the flood— Is it an eagle or a fish-hawk?— Ah, now he is betrayed, I know not by what motion—a great gull.— right in the eye of the storm— He holds not a steady course—but suddenly he dashes upward even like the surf of the sea which he frequents—showing the under sides of his long, pointed wings. . . . He suddenly beats upward . . . as if to surmount the airy billows by a slanting course as the teamster surmounts a slope. The swallow too flys fantastically & . . . luxuriously & leisurely—doubling some unseen corners in the sky. Here is a gull then long after ice in the river. It is a fine sight to see this noble bird leisurely advancing right in the face of the storm.

Spring

How sweet is the perception of a new natural fact!—suggesting what worlds remain to be unveiled. . . . To see the larger & wilder birds you must go forth in the great storms like this. At such times they frequent our neighborhood & trust themselves in our midst. A life of fair weather walks *might* never show you the goose sailing on our waters, or the Great Heron feeding here. When the storm increases then these great birds that carry the mail of the seasons lay to. To see wild life—you must go forth at a wild season. When it rains & blows keeping men in-doors then the lover of nature must [go] forth. Then returns nature to her wild estate.

19 April 1852, Journal *4:470–73*

❦ IT IS VERY RARE that I hear one express a strong and imperishable attachment to a particular scenery, or to the whole of nature,—I mean such as will control their whole lives and characters. Such seem to have a true home in nature, a hearth in the fields and woods, whatever tenement may be burned. The soil and climate [are] warm to them. They alone are naturalized, but most are tender and callow creatures that wear a house as their outmost shell and must get their lives insured when they step abroad from it. They are lathed and plastered in from all natural influences, and their delicate lives are a long battle with dyspepsia. The others are fairly rooted in the soil, and are the noblest plant it bears, more hardy and natural than sorrel. The dead earth seems animated at the prospect of their coming, as if proud to be trodden on by them. It recognizes its lord. Children of the Golden Age. Hospitals and almshouses are not their destiny. When I hear of such an attachment in a reasonable, a divine, creature to a particular portion of the earth, it seems as if then first the earth succeeded and rejoiced, as if it had been made and existed only for such a use. These various soils and reaches which the farmer plods over, which the traveller glances at and the geologist dryly describes, then first flower and bear their fruit. Does he chiefly own the land who coldly uses it and gets corn and potatoes out of it, or he who loves it and gets inspiration from it? How rarely a man's love for nature becomes a ruling principle with him, like a youth's affection for a maiden, but more enduring! All nature is my bride. That nature which to one is a stark and ghastly solitude is a sweet, tender, and genial society to another.

23 April 1857, Journal *IX:336–37*

❦ THIS SEASON OF RAIN and superabundant moisture makes attractive many an unsightly hollow and recess. I see some roadside lakes, where the grass and clover had already sprung, owing to previous rain or melted snow, now filled with perfectly transparent April rain-water, through which I see to their emerald bottoms,—paved with emerald. In the pasture beyond Nut Meadow Crossing, the unsightly holes where rocks have been dug and blasted out are now converted into perfect jewels. They are filled with water of crystalline transparency, paved with the same emerald, with a few hardhacks and meadow-sweets standing in them, and jagged points of rock, and a few skaters gliding over them. Even these furnish goblets and vases of perfect purity to hold the dews and rains, and what more agreeable bottom can we look to than this which the earliest moisture and sun had tinged green? We do not object to see dry leaves and withered grass at the bottom of the goblet when we drink, if these manifestly do not affect the purity of the water. What wells can be more charming? If I see an early grasshopper drowning in one, it looks like a fate to be envied. Here is no dark unexplored bottom, with its imagined monsters and mud, but perfect sincerity, setting off all that it reveals. Through this medium we admire even the decaying leaves and sticks at the bottom. . . .

April wells, call them.

24 April 1856, Journal *VIII:304–5*

❦ THERE IS A SEASON for everything, and we do not notice a given phenomenon except at that season, if, indeed, it can be called the same phenomenon at any other season. There is a time to watch the ripples on Ripple Lake, to look for arrowheads, to study the rocks and lichens, a time to walk on sandy deserts; and the observer of nature must improve these seasons as much as the farmer his. So boys fly kites and play ball or hawkie at particular times all over the State. A wise man will know what game to play to-day, and play it. We must not be governed by rigid rules, as by the almanac, but let the season rule us. The moods and thoughts of man are revolving just as steadily and incessantly as nature's. Nothing must be postponed. Take time by the forelock. Now or never! You must live in the present, launch yourself on every wave, find your eternity in each moment. Fools stand on their island opportunities and look toward another land. There is no other land; there is no other life but this, or the like of this. Where the good husbandman is, there is the good soil. Take any other course, and life will be a succession of regrets. Let us see vessels sailing prosperously before the wind, and not simply stranded barks. There is no world for the penitent and regretful.

24 April 1859, Journal *XII:159–60*

❦ IT IS FOOLISH for a man to accumulate material wealth chiefly, houses and land. Our stock in life, or real estate, is that amount of thought which we have had, which we have thought out. The ground we have thus created is forever pasturage for our thoughts. I fall back on to visions which I have had. What else adds to my possessions and makes me rich in all lands? If you have ever done any work with these finest tools, the imagination and fancy and reason, it is a new creation, independent of the world, and a possession forever. You have laid up something against a rainy day. You have to that extent cleared the wilderness.

1 May 1857, Journal *IX:350*

❦ THERE IS NO such thing as pure *objective* observation— You[r] observation—to be interesting[,] i.e. to be significant must be *subjective* The sum of what the writer of whatever class has to report is simply some human experience—whether he be poet or philosopher or man of science— The man of most science is the man most alive—whose life is the greatest event—senses that take cognizance of outward things merely are of no avail. It matters not where or how far you travel—the farther commonly the worse—but how much alive you are. If it is possible to conceive of an event outside to humanity—it is not of the slightest significance—though it were the explosion of a planet— Every important worker will report what life there is in him— It makes no odds into what seeming deserts the poet is born. Though all his neighbors pronounce it a Sahara—it will be a paradise to him—for the desert which we see is the re[s]ult of the barrenness of our experience. No mere wilful

activity whatever—whether in writing verses or collecting sta-
tistics will produce true poetry or science— If you are really a
sick man it is indeed to be regretted for you cannot accomplish
so much as if you were well. All that a man has to say or do
that can possibly concern mankind, is in some shape or other
to tell the story of his love— And if he is fortunate an[d] keeps
alive he will be forever in love— This alone is to be alive to the
extremeties—

6 May 1854, Journal 8:98

❧ THERE IS A *positive* sweetness in the air from flowers &
expanding leaves—a universal sweetness— A longish yellow
abdomened bee. Chicadee's phoebe note is common now—the
tull a lull more rare & in mornings. It is impossible to remember a week ago— A river of lethe flows with many windings
the year through—separating one season from another. The
heavens for a few days have been lost[;] it has been a sort of
paradise instead. As with the seashore so is it with the universal
earth-shore, not in summer can you look far in to the ocean of
the ether. They who come to this world as to a watering place
in the summer for coolness & luxury never get the far & fine
november views of heaven.

Is not all the summer akin to a paradise—we have to bathe in
ponds to brace ourselves—

9 May 1852, Journal 5:47

❦ WHILE DROPPING BEANS in the garden . . . just after sundown
. . . I hear from across the fields the note of the bay-wing, *Come
here here there there quick quick quick or I'm gone* (which I have no
doubt sits on some fence-post or rail there), and it instantly
translates me from the sphere of my work and repairs all the
world that we jointly inhabit. It reminds me of so many country
afternoons and evenings when this bird's strain was heard far
over the fields, as I pursued it from field to field. The spirit of its
earth-song, of its serene and true philosophy, was breathed into
me, and I saw the world as through a glass, as it lies eternally.
Some of its aboriginal contentment, even of its domestic felicity,
possessed me. What he suggests is permanently true. As the
bay-wing sang many a thousand years ago, so sang he to-night.
In the beginning God heard his song and pronounced it good,
and hence it has endured. It reminded me of many a summer
sunset, of many miles of gray rails, of many a rambling pasture,
of the farmhouse far in the fields, its milk-pans and well-sweep,
and the cows coming home from pasture.

I would thus from time to time take advice of the birds, correct
my human views by listening to their volucral. He is a brother
poet, this small gray bird (or bard), whose muse inspires mine.
His lay is an idyl or pastoral, older and sweeter than any that
is classic. He sits on some gray perch like himself, on a stake,
perchance, in the midst of the field, and you can hardly see him
against the plowed ground. You advance step by step as the
twilight deepens, and lo! he is gone, and in vain you strain your
eyes to see whither, but anon his tinkling strain is heard from
some other quarter. One with the rocks and with us.

Methinks I hear these sounds, have these reminiscences, only
when well employed, at any rate only when I have no reason to
be ashamed of my employment. I am often aware of a certain

compensation of this kind for doing something from a sense of duty, even unconsciously. Our past experience is a never-failing capital which can never be alienated, of which each kindred future event reminds us. If you would have the song of the sparrow inspire you a thousand years hence, let your life be in harmony with its strain to-day.

12 May 1857, Journal *IX:363–64*

❧ THE FIRST CRICKETS chirrup which I have chanced to hear now falls on my ear—& makes me forget all else—all else is a thin & movable crust down to that depth where he resides eternally. He already fore tels autumn—deep under the dry border of some rock in this hillside he sits & makes the finest singing of birds outward & insignificant—his own song is so much deeper & more significant. His voice has set me thinking—philosophizing—moralizing at once—it is not so wildly melodious but it is wiser & more mature than that of the wood thrush—with this elixir I see clear through the summer now to autumn & any summer work seems frivolous— I am disposed to ask this humble bee that hurries humming past so busily—if he knows what he is about?— At one leap I go from the just opened buttercup to the life[-]everlasting. This singer has antedated autumn. His strain is superior . . . to seasons. It annihilates time & space—the summer is for time servers.

15 May 1853, Journal *6:124*

❦ I SIT NOW ON A ROCK on the w[est] slope of Fair Haven orchard—an hour before sunset this warm almost sultry evening—the air filled with the sweetness of apple blossoms . . . or I think it is mainly meadow fragrance still—the sun partly concealed behind a low cloud in the west—the air cleared by last evening's thunder shower—the river now beautifully smooth . . . full of light & reflecting the placid western sky & the dark woods which overhang it— I was surprised on turning round to behold the serene & everlasting beauty of the world—it was so soothing— I saw that I could not go home to supper & lose it.— It was so much fairer[,] serener[,] more beautiful than my mood had been. The fields beyond the river have unexpectedly—a smooth lawn like beauty & in beautiful curves sweep round the edge of the woods. The rapidly expanding foliage of the deciduous [trees] . . . lights up with a lively yellow green the dark pines which we have so long been used to— Some patches (I speak of woods ½ mile or more off) are a lively green—some gray or reddish gray still—where white oaks stand. With the stillness of the air comes the stillness of the water—the sweetest singers among the birds are heard more distinctly now as the reflections are seen more distinctly in the water—the veery constantly now— Methinks this serene ambrosial beauty could hardly have been but for last evening's thunder shower—which to be sure barely touched us—but cleared the air & gave a start to vegetation. The elm on the opposite side of the river has now a thin but dark verdure almost as dark as the pines—while . . . the prevailing color of the deciduous woods is a light yellowish & sunny green— The woods rarely if ever present a more beautiful aspect from afar than now. Methinks the black oak at early leafing is more red than the red oak. Ah the beauty of this last hour of the day when a power stills the air & smooths all waters & all minds— . . . Sit on [the] Cliffs. . . . The perfect smoothness of Fair Haven Pond—full of light & reflecting the woods distinctly—while still occasionally the sun shines warm & brightly from behind a cloud—giving the completest contrast of sunshine & shade—are enough to make this hour memorable. . . .

Returning [home] slowly I sit on the wall of the orchard by the White Pine. Now the cows begin to low—& the river reflects the golden light of the sun just before his setting. The sough of the wind in the pines is more noticeable as if the air were otherwise more still & hollow. The wood thrush has sung for sometime. He touches a depth in me which no other birds song does. He has learned to sing & no thrumming of the strings or tuning disturbs you. Other birds may whistle pretty well but he is the master of a finer toned instrument. His song is musical not from association merely—not from variety but from the character of its tone. It is all divine—a Shakspeare among birds & a Homer too. . . .

The fragrance of the apple-blossom—reminds me of a pure & innocent & unsophisticated country girl—bedecked for church. The purple sunset—is reflected from the surface of the river as if its surface were tinged with a *lake*. Here is a field sparrow that varies his strain very sweetly. . . . The Beach Plum is out *today*. The Whipporwill sings— Large insects now fly at night— . . . The lilac is out.

Genius rises above nature, in spite of heat—in spite of cold— works & lives—

17 May 1853, Journal *6:131–34*

❦ THE POET must bring to nature the smooth mirror in which she is to be reflected. He must be something superior to her[,] something more than universal. . . .

. . . It is glorious to stand in the midst of the andromedas[,] which so level and thick fills the swamp—& look up at the blue spruce trees—the edges of the scales of the young cones which are at the tops of the trees—(where the branches make light & open crosses—) seen against the sun-lit sky or against the light merely[,] being transparent—and a splendid crimson color—as if the condensed fire of all sunsets were reflected from them— . . . [T]hey glow with the crimson fires of the sunset sky—reflected over the swamp[—]unspeakably rare & precious rubies as you thus look up at them, but climb the tree & look down on them & they are comparatively dull & opaque. These are the rubies of the swamp— Already the just-bursting leaf buds emit that rare strawberry fragrance. It is one of the most glowing[,] beautiful[,] brilliant effects in nature[,] exactly like the reflections from the breast of the ruby throated humming birds—as if a hundred ruby throated hummingbirds sat on the topmost crosses of the trees[,] their breasts turned to the sun. . . . How different the ram-rod jingle of the che-wink or any bird's note sounds now at 5 Pm in the cooler[,] stiller air—when also the humming of insects is more distinctly heard & perchance some impurity has begun to sink to earth strained by the air. Or is it perchance to be referred to the cooler more clarified & pensive state of the mind—when dews have begun to descend in it & clarify it? A certain lateness in the sound—pleasing to the ear—which releases me from the obligation to return in any particular season— I have passed the Rubicon of staying out— I have said to my self that way is not homeward— I will wander further from what I have called my home[—]to the home which is forever inviting me. In such an hour the freedom of the woods is offered me—and the birds sing my dispensation. In dreams the links of life are united—we forget that our friends are dead—we know them as of old.

23 May 1853, Journal *6:145–8*

❦ SOME INCIDENTS in my life have seemed far more allegorical than actual—they were so significant that they plainly served no other use. That is[,] I have been more impressed by their allegorical significance & fitness—they have been like myths or passages in a myth—rather than mere incidents or history which have to wait to become significant. Quite in harmony with my subjective philosophy— This for instance—that, when I thought I knew the flowers so well the beautiful purple azalea or pinxter-flower should be shown me by the hunter who found it. Such facts are lifted quite above the level of the actual. They are all just such events as my imagination prepares me for—no matter how incredible— Perfectly in keeping with my life & characteristic— Ever and anon something will occur which my philosophy has not dreamed of. The limits of the actual are set some thoughts further off. That which had seemed a rigid wall of vast thickness unexpectedly proves a thin and undulating drapery—the boundaries of the actual are no more fixed & rigid—than the elasticity of our imaginations. The fact that a rare & beautiful flower which we never saw—perhaps never heard [of—] for which therefore there was no place in our thoughts may at length be found in our immediate neighborhood, is very suggestive.

31 May 1853, Journal *6:162*

❧ WITHIN LITTLE MORE than a fortnight the woods from bare twigs have become a Sea of verdure—& young *shoots* have contended with one another in the race. The leaves have unfurled all over the country like an umbrella—shade is produced—& the birds are concealed—& their economies go forward uninterruptedly—and a covert is afforded to the animals generally— Myriads of little parasols are suddenly spread all the country over to shield the earth & the roots of the trees from parching heat—& they begin to flutter & rustle in the breeze.

1 June 1854, Journal *8:170*

❧ IT HAS JUST CLEARED off after this first rain of consequence for a long time, and now I observe the shadows of massive clouds still floating here and there in the peculiarly blue sky; which dark shadows on field and wood are the more remarkable by contrast with the light yellow-green foliage now, and when they rest on evergreens they are doubly dark, like dark rings about the eyes of June. Great white-bosomed clouds, darker beneath, float through the cleared sky and are seen against the deliciously blue sky, such a sky as we have not had before. Thus it is after the first important rain at this season. The song of birds is more lively and seems to have a new character; a new season has commenced.

4 June 1855, Journal *VII:404*

Spring

❧ THE LUPINE is now in its glory. It is the more important because it occurs in such extensive patches even an acre or more together—and of such a pleasing variety of colors, purple—pink or lilac—and white—especially with the sun on it, when the transparency of the flower makes its color changeable. It paints a whole hill side with its blue—making such a field—(if not a meadow) as Proserpine might have wandered in. Its leaf was made to be covered with dew drops— I am quite excited by this prospect of blue flowers in clumps with narrow intervals— Such a profusion of the heavenly—the elysian color—as if these were the elysian fields. They say the seeds look like babies' faces and hence the flower is so named. No other flowers exhibit so much blue. That is the value of the lupine The earth is blued with them. Yet a third of a mile distant I do not detect their color on the hill side— Perchance because it is the color of the air. It is not *distinct* enough. You passed along here perchance a fortnight ago & the hill-side was comparatively barren—but now you come & these glorious redeemers appear to have flashed out here all at once. Who planted the seeds of lupines in the barren soil? Who watereth the lupines in the fields?

5 June 1852, Journal *5:79–80*

❧ THIS IS JUNE, the month of grass and leaves. The deciduous trees are investing the evergreens and revealing how dark they are. Already the aspens are trembling again, and a new summer is offered me. I feel a little fluttered in my thoughts, as if I might be too late. Each season is but an infinitesimal point. It no sooner comes than it is gone. It has no duration. It simply gives a tone and hue to my thought. Each annual phenomenon is a reminiscence and prompting. Our thoughts and sentiments answer to the revolutions of the seasons, as two cog-wheels fit into each other. We are conversant with only one point of contact at a time, from which we receive a prompting and impulse and instantly pass to a new season or point of contact. A year is made up of a certain series and number of sensations and thoughts which have their language in nature. Now I am ice, now I am sorrel. Each experience reduces itself to a mood of the mind.

6 June 1857, Journal *IX:406–7*

It is a certain faery land where we live—you may walk out in any direction over the earth's surface—lifting your horizon—and every where your path—climbing the convexity of the globe leads you between heaven & earth— —not away from the light of the sun & stars—& the habitations of men. I wonder that I even get 5 miles on my way—the walk is so crowded with events—& phenomena. How many questions there are which I have not put to the inhabitants!

7 June 1851, Journal *3:245*

The life in us is like the water in the river, it may rise this year higher than ever it was known to before and flood the uplands—even this may be the eventful year—& drown out all our muskrats There are as many strata at different levels of life as there are leaves in a book Most men probably have lives in two or three. When on the higher levels we can remember the lower levels, but when on the lower we cannot remember the higher.

My imagination, my love & reverence & admiration, my sense of the miraculous is not so excited by any event as by the remembrance of my youth. Men talk about bible miracles because there is no miracle in their lives. Cease to gnaw that crust. There is ripe fruit over your head

9 June 1850, Journal *3:84*

❦ FOR A WEEK PAST we have had *washing* days— The grass waving and trees having leafed out their boughs wave and feel the effect on the breeze. Thus new life & motion is imparted to the trees— The season of waving boughs—and the lighter under sides of the new leaves are exposed. This is the first half of June. Already the grass is not so fresh & liquid velvety a green—having much of it blossom & some even gone to seed— & it is mixed with reddish ferns & other plants—but the general leafiness—shadiness & waving of grass & boughs in the breeze characterize the season. The wind is not quite agreeable— because it prevents your hearing the birds sing. Meanwhile the crickets are strengthening their quire. The weather is very clear & the sky bright. The river shines like silver. Methinks this is a traveller's month. The locust in bloom— The waving undulating rye. The deciduous trees have filled up the intervals between the . . . evergreens. & the woods are bosky now.

9 June 1852, Journal *5:81-82*

❦ WALKED TO WALDEN last night (moon not quite full) by railroad & upland wood path, returning by Wayland Road. Last full moon the elms had not leaved out, cast no heavy shadows & their outlines were less striking & rich in the streets at night. . . . I noticed a night before night before last from Fair Haven how valuable was some water by moonlight like the river & Fair Haven pond though far away—reflecting the light with a faint glimmering sheen, as in the spring of the year The water shines with an inward light like a heaven on earth. The silent depth & serenity & majesty of water—strange that men should distinguish gold & diamonds—when these precious elements are so common. I saw a distant river by moon light making no noise, yet flowing as by day—still to the sea, like melted silver reflecting the moon light—far away it lay encircling the earth How far away it may look in the night and even from a low hill how miles away down in the valley! As far off . . . as Paradise and the delectable country! There is a certain glory attended on water by night. By it the heavens are related to the earth— Undistinguishable from a sky beneath you—

And I forgot to say that after I reach the road by Potters barns— . . . I saw the moon sudden reflected full from a pool— A puddle from which you may see the moon reflected—& the earth dissolved under your feet.

The magical moon with attendant stars suddenly looking up with mild lustre from a window in the dark earth.

13 June 1851, Journal *3:259-60*

❦ WHERE THE most beautiful wild flowers grow—there Man's spirit is fed—& poets grow—

15 June 1852, Journal *5:100*

Spring

❦ Would it not be a luxury to stand up to ones chin in some retired swamp for a whole summer's day, scenting the sweet fern and bilberry blows, and lulled by the minstrelsy of gnats and mosquitoes? A day passed in the society of those Greek sages, such as described in the "Banquet" of Xenophon, would not be comparable with the dry wit of decayed cranberry vines, and the fresh Attic salt of the moss beds. Say twelve hours of genial and familiar converse with the leopard frog. The sun to rise behind alder and dogwood, and climb boyantly to his meridian of three hands' breadth—and finally sink to rest behind some bold western hummock. To hear the evening chant of the mosquito from a thousand green chapels—and the bittern begin to boom from his concealed fort—like a sunset gun!

Surely, one may as profitably be soaked in the juices of a marsh for one day, as pick his way dry shod over sand. Cold and damp—are they not as rich experience as warmth and dryness?

So is not Shade as good as sunshine—Night as day? Why be eagles and thrushes always, and owls and whip-poor-wills never[?]

16 June 1840, Journal *1:129*

SUMMER

Nature has looked uncommonly bare & dry to me for a day or two. With our senses applied to the surrounding world we are reading our own physical & corresponding moral revolutions. Nature was so shallow all at once I did not know what had attracted me all my life. I was therefore encouraged when going through a field this evening, I was unexpectedly struck with the beauty of an apple tree— The perception of beauty is a moral test.

21 June 1852, Journal *5:120*

❦ As I come over the hill, I hear the wood thrush singing his evening lay. This is the only bird whose note affects me like music, affects the flow and tenor of my thought, my fancy and imagination. It lifts and exhilarates me. It is inspiring. It is a medicative draught to my soul. It is an elixir to my eyes and a fountain of youth to all my senses. It changes all hours to an eternal morning. It banishes all trivialness. It reinstates me in my dominion, makes me the lord of creation, is chief musician of my court. This minstrel sings in a time, a heroic age, with which no event in the village can be contemporary. How can they be contemporary when only the latter is *temporary* at all? How can the infinite and eternal be contemporary with the finite and temporal? So there is something in the music of the cow-bell, something sweeter and more nutritious, than in the milk which the farmers drink. This thrush's song is a *ranz des vaches* to me. I long for wildness, a nature which I cannot put my foot through, woods where the wood thrush forever sings, where the hours are early morning ones, and there is dew on the grass, and the day is forever unproved, where I might have a fertile unknown for a soil about me. I would go after the cows, I would watch the flocks of Admetus there forever, only for my board and clothes. A New Hampshire everlasting and unfallen.

How wonderfully moral our whole life! There is never an instant's truce between virtue and vice. Goodness is the only investment that never fails. It is sung of in the music of the harp. This it is which thrills us. The harp is the travelling patterer for the Universe Insurance Company. Our little goodness is all the assessment.

All that was ripest and fairest in the wilderness and the wild man is preserved and transmitted to us in the strain of the wood thrush. It is the mediator between barbarism and civilization.

22 June 1853, Journal *V:292-93*

❦ A HEALTHY & REFINED NATURE would always derive pleasure from the landscape. As long as the bodily vigor lasts, man sympathizes with nature— . . .

Saw a very large white ash tree 3 1/2 feet in diameter in front of the house which White formerly owned under this hill— which was struck by lightning. . . . The lightning apparently struck the top of the tree & scorched the bark & leaves for 10 or 15 feet downward—then began to strip off the bark & enter the wood, making a ragged narrow furrow or crack—till reaching one of the upper limbs it apparently divided—descending on both sides & entering deeper & deeper into the wood. At the first general branching it had got full possession of the tree in its center—and tossed off the main limbs butt foremost making holes in the ground where they struck—& so it went down in the midst of the trunk to the earth where it apparently exploded, rending the trunk into six segments, whose tops 10 or 20 feet long were rayed out on every side at an angle . . . leaving the ground bare directly under where the tree had stood, though they were still fastened to the earth by their roots. The lightning appeared to have gone off through the roots, furrowing them as branches, and through the earth, making a furrow like a plough 4 or 5 rods in one direction & in another passing through the cellar of the neighboring house, about 30 feet distant—scorching the tin milk pans & throwing dirt into the milk & coming out the back side of the house—in a furrow—splitting some planks there— The main body of the tree was completely stripped of bark—which was cast in every direction 2 hundred feet. . . . The heart of the tree lay by itself— Probably a piece as large as [a] man's leg could not have been sawed out of the trunk which would not have had a crack in it—& much of it was very finely splintered.

The windows in the house were broken & the inhabitants knocked down by the concussion. All this was accomplished in an instant by a kind of fire out of the heavens. . . . For what purpose? The ancients called it Joves bolt—with which he punished the guilty—& we moderns understand it no better. There was displayed a Titanic force—some of that force which made and can unmake the world. The brute forces are not yet wholly tamed. Is this of the character of a wild beast—or is it guided by intelligence and mercy? If we trust our natural impressions it is a manifestation of brutish force—or vengeance more or less tempered with justice. Yet it is our own consciousness of sin probably which suggests the idea of vengeance—and to a righteous-man it would be mere sublime without being aweful.

. . . In a violent tempest, we both fear & trust. We are ashamed
of our fear for we know that a righteous man would not suspect danger—nor incur any. Wherever a man feels fear, there
is an avenger— The savage's & the civilized man's instincts are
right. Science affirms too much. Science assumes to show *why*
the lightning strikes a tree—but it does not show us the moral
why, any better than our instincts did. It is full of presumption.
Why should trees be struck? It is not enough to say because
they are in the way. Science answers *non scio*—I am ignorant.
All the phenomena of nature need be seen from the point of
view of wonder & awe—like lightning—& on the other hand
the lightning itself needs to [be] regarded with serenety as the
most familiar & innocent phenomena. There runs through the
righteous man's moral spine—a rod with burnished points to
heaven which conducts safely away in to the earth the flash-
ing wrath of Nemesis—so that it merely clarifies the air. This
moment the confidence of the righteous man erects a sure con-
ductor within him—

27 June 1852, Journal *5:157-60*

❦ I SAILED FROM FAIR HAVEN last evening as gently and
steadily as the clouds sail through the atmosphere. The wind
came blowing blithely from the South west fields, and stepped
into the folds of our sail like a winged horse—pulling with a
strong and steady impulse. The sail bends gently to the breeze
as swells some generous impulse of the heart—and anon flut-
ters and flaps with a kind of human suspense. I could watch the
motions of a sail forever, they are so rich and full of meaning.
I watch the play of its pulse as if it were my own blood beat-
ing there. The varying temperature of distant atmospheres is

graduated on its scale. It is a free boyant creature—the bauble of the heavens and the earth. A gay pastime the air plays with it. If it swells and tugs, it is because the sun lays his windy finger on it.— — The breeze it plays with has been outdoors so long— So thin is it—and yet so full of life. So noiseless when it labors hardest—so noisy and impatient when least servicible. So am I blown on by God's breath— So flutter and flap, and fill gently out with the breeze.

In this fresh evening each blade and leaf looks as if it had been dipped in an icy liquid greenness. Let eyes that ache come here and look, the sight will be a sovereign eye water, or else wait and bathe there in the dark.

30 June 1840, Journal *1:145*

❧ NATURE MUST BE VIEWED humanly to be viewed at all—that is her scenes must be associated with humane affections—such as are associated with ones native place for instance. She is most significant to a lover. A lover of nature is preeminently a lover of man. If I have no friend—what is nature to me? She ceases to be morally significant.

30 June 1852, Journal *5:164*

❧ A. M.— START FOR WHITE MOUNTAINS. . . .

Spent the noon close by the old Dunstable graveyard. . . . Red lilies were abundantly in bloom in the burying-ground and by the river. . . .

Walked to and along the river and bathed in it. . . .

What a relief and expansion of my thoughts when I come
out from that inland position by the graveyard to this broad
river's shore! This vista was incredible there. Suddenly I see
a broad reach of blue beneath, with its curves and headlands,
liberating me from the more terrene earth. What a difference
it makes whether I spend my four hours' nooning between the
hills by yonder roadside, or on the brink of this fair river, within
a quarter of a mile of that! Here the earth is fluid to my thought,
the sky is reflected from beneath, and around yonder cape is
the highway to other continents. This current allies me to all
the world. Be careful to sit in an elevating and inspiring place.
There my thoughts were confined and trivial, and I hid myself
from the gaze of travellers. Here they are expanded and ele-
vated, and I am charmed by the beautiful river-reach. It is equal
to a different season and country and creates a different mood.
As you travel northward from Concord, probably the reaches
of the Merrimack River, looking up or down them from the
bank, will be the first inspiring sight. There is something in the
scenery of a broad river equivalent to culture and civilization.
Its channel conducts our thoughts as well as bodies to classic
and famous ports, and allies us to all that is fair and great. I like
to remember that at the end of half a day's walk I can stand on
the bank of the Merrimack. It is just wide enough to interrupt
the land and lead my eye and thoughts down its channel to the
sea. A river is superior to a lake in its liberating influence. It
has motion and indefinite length. A river touching the back of a
town is like a wing, it may be unused as yet, but ready to waft it
over the world. With its rapid current it is a slightly fluttering
wing. River towns are winged towns.

2 July 1858, Journal *XI:3–5*

❦ THE PROGRESS of the season is indescribable— It is growing warm again—but the warmth is different from that we have had— We lie in the shade of locust trees—haymakers go by in a hay-rigging— I am reminded of berrying— I scent the sweet fern & the dead or dry pine leaves—cherry-birds alight on a neighboring tree. The warmth is something more normal—& steady—ripening fruits. . . .

. . . It begins to be such weather as when people go a huckleberrying. Nature offers fruits now as well as flowers— We have become accustomed to the summer— It has acquired a certain eternity— . . . Some birds are poets & sing all summer—they are the true singers— Any man can write verses during the love season— I am reminded of this while [I] rest in the shade on the Maj. Heywood road—& listen to a wood thrush now just before sunset— We are most interested in those birds who sing for the love of music and not of their mates—who meditate their strains and *amuse* themselves with singing— The birds— the—strains of deeper sentiment—not bobolinks that lose their plumage their bright colors & their song so early.

. . . The thrush alone declares the immortal wealth & vigor that is in the forest— Here is a bird in whose strain the story is told—though Nature waited for the science of aesthetics to discover it to man. Whenever a man hears it he is young— & nature is in her spring— Whenever he hears it it is a new world—and a free country—and the gates of heaven are not shut against him— Most other birds sing from the level of my ordinary cheerful hours—a carol—but this bird never fails to speak to me out of an ether purer than that I breathe—of immortal beauty & vigor— He deepens the significance of all things seen in the light of his strain. He sings to make men take higher and truer views of things. He sings to amend their institutions. To relieve the slave on the plantation—& the prisoner in his dungeon—the slave in the house of luxury & the prisoner of his own low thoughts.

How fitting to have every day in a vase of water on your table the wild flowers of the season—which are just blossoming—can any house [be] said to be furnished without them? Shall we be so forward to pluck the fruits of nature—& neglect her flowers? These are surely her finest influences So may the season suggest the fine thoughts it is fitted to suggest. Shall we say "A penny for your thoughts"—before we have looked in the face of nature. Let me know what picture she is painting—what poetry she is writing—what ode composing now.

5 July 1852, Journal *5:185–88*

❦ 4 A.M. The first really foggy morning yet before I rise I hear the song of birds from out it—like the bursting of its bubbles with music—the head on liquids just uncorked. Their song gilds thus the frost work of the morning— As if the fog were a great sweet froth on the surface of land and water—whose fixed air escaped—whose bubbles burst with music. The sound of its evaporation—the fixed air of the morning just brought from the cellars of the night escaping.— The morning twittering of birds in perfect harmony with it. I came near awaking this morning. I am older than last year[;] the mornings are further between— The days are fewer— Any excess . . . is fatal to the morning's clarity—but in health the sound of a cow bell is celestial music. O might I always wake to thought & poetry—regenerated! Can [it] be called a morning—if our senses are not clarified so that we perceive more clearly—if we do not rise with elastic vigor? How wholesome these fogs which some fear—they are cool medicated vapor baths—mingled by nature which bring to our senses all the medical properties of the meadows. The touchstones of health— . . . To the Cliffs— The fog condenses into fountains & streams of music as in the strain of the bobolink which I hear—& runs off so—the music of the birds is the tinkling of the rills that flow from it. I cannot see 20 rods The trees look darker through it & their outlines more distinct apparently because of the whiteness of the fog— and the less light that comes through the trees. There is every where dew on the cobwebs—little gossamer veils or scarfs as big as your hand dropped from the fairy shoulders that danced on the grass the past night— . . . these dewy webs are as thick as anywhere—promising a fair day—

7 July 1852, Journal *5:194–95*

❦ I HEAR THE SOUND of Heywood's brook falling into Fair Haven Pond—inexpressibly refreshing to my senses—it seems to flow through my very bones.— I hear it with insatiable thirst— It allays some sandy heat in me— It affects my circulations—methinks my arteries have sympathy with it What is it I hear but the pure water falls within me in the circulation of my blood—the streams that fall into my heart?— what mists do I ever see but such as hang over—& rise from my blood— The sound of this gurgling water—running thus by night as by day—falls on all my dashes—fills all my buckets—overflows my float boards—turns all the machinery of my nature[,] makes me a flume—a sluice way to the springs of nature— Thus I am washed thus I drink—& quench my thirst.

11 July 1851, Journal *3:301*

❦ THE RIVER IS LOW. Now is the time for meadow walking . . . You go dry shod now through meadows which were comparatively impassable before. Those western reserves which you had not explored. We are thankful that the water has preserved them inviolate so long. There is a cheerful light reflected from the undersides of the ferns in the dryer meadows now— . . . especially in breezy weather. It was so in June. The dusty roads & roadsides begin to show the effects of drouth— The corn rolls. The bass on Conantum is now well in blossom. . . . Its flowers are conspicuous for a tree & a rather agreeable odor fills the air. The tree resounds with the hum of bees on the flowers On the whole it is a rich sight. . . . How valuable & significant is shade now— Trees appear valuable for shade mainly—& we observe their shadows as much as their form & foliage. The waving of the meadow grass near Fair Haven Isle—is very agreeable & refreshing to one looking down from an elevation. It appears not merely like a waving—or undulation but a progress a creeping as of an invisible army over it—its flat curly head. The grass appears tufted—*watered*. On the river the ripple is continued into the pads—where it is smoother—a longer undulation. Pines or evergreens do not attract so much attention now. They have retired on the laurels of the winter. What is called genius is the abundance of life or health so that whatever addresses the senses—as the flavor of these berries— or the lowing of that cow—which sounds as if it echoed along a cool *mt*side just before night—where odoriferous dews perfume the air and there is everlasting vigor[,] serenity—& expectation of perpetual untarnished morning—each sight & sound & scent & flavor—intoxicates with a healthy intoxication— The shrunken stream of life overflows its banks[,] makes & fertilizes broad intervals from which generations derive their sustenances. This is the true overflowing of the Nile. So exquisitely sensitive are we— It makes us embrace our fates & instead of suffering or indifference, we enjoy & bless. If we have not dissipated the vital[,] the divine fluids—then is there a circulation of vitality beyond our bodies. The cow is nothing— Heaven is not there—but in the condition of the hearer—

11 July 1852, Journal *5:214–15*

❦ MANY MEN walk by day[,] few walk by night. It is a very different season. Instead of the sun there are the moon & stars—instead of the wood thrush there is the whippoorwill—instead of butter flies[,] fire flies winged sparks of fire—for every thing has wings set to it at last—instead of singing birds the croaking of frogs & the intenser dream of crickets— The potatoes stand up straight—the corn grows—the bushes loom—& in a moon-light night the shadows of rocks—& trees & bushes & hills—are are more conspicuous than the objects themselves. The slightest inequalities in the ground are revealed by the shadows—what the feet find comparatively smooth appears rough & diversified to the eye. The smallest recesses in the rocks are dim & cavernous—the ferns in the wood appear to be of tropical size—the pools become as full of light as the sky. The roads are heavy & dark. Nature slumbers The rocks retain the warmth of the sun which they have absorbed all night—

After 16 July 1850, Journal *3:92*

❦ REMEMBER THY CREATOR in the days of thy youth. i.e. Lay up a store of natural influences—sing while you may before the evil days come—he that hath ears let him hear—see—hear—smell—taste—&c while these senses are fresh & pure

There is always a kind of fine Æolian harp music to be heard
in the air— I hear now as it were the mellow sound of distant horns in the hollow mansions of the upper air—a sound to
make all men divinely insane that hear it—far away over head
subsiding into my ear. [To] ears that are expanded what a harp
this world is!

21 July 1851, Journal *3:323*

❦ A COMFORTABLE BREEZE BLOWING. Methinks I can write
better in the afternoon, for the novelty of it—if I should go
abroad this morning— My genius makes distinctions which my
understanding can not—and which my senses do not report.
If I should reverse the usual, go forth & saunter in the fields
all the forenoon then sit down in my chamber in the afternoon
which it is so unusual for me to do—it would be like a new
season to me & the novelty of it inspire me. The wind has fairly
blown me out doors—the elements were so lively & active—&
I so sympathized with them that I could not sit while the wind
went by. And I am reminded that we should especially improve
the summer to live out of doors— When we may so easily it
behoves us to break up this custom of sitting in the house. for
it is but a custom—and I am not sure that it has the sanction
of common sense. A man no sooner gets up than he sits down
again. . . . Is the literary man to live always or chiefly sitting in
a chamber—through which Nature enters by a window only?
What is the use of summer?

You must walk so gently as to hear the finest sounds—the
faculties being in repose— Your mind must not perspire True,
out of doors my thought is commonly drowned as it were &
shrunken pressed down by stupendous piles of light etherial
influences—for the pressure of the atmosphere is still 15 lbs to a

square inch— I can do little more than preserve the equilibrium & resist the pressure of the atmosphere— I can only nod like the rye-heads in the breeze.— I expand more surely in my chamber—as far as expression goes, as if that pressure were taken off.— but here outdoors is the place to store up influences . . .

The influences which make for one walk more than another & one day more than another—one much more etherial than terrestrial. It is the quality of the air much more than the quality of the ground that concerns the walker[,] cheers or depresses him. . . .

The mind is subject to moods as the shadows of clouds pass over the earth— Pay not too much heed to them— Let not the traveller stop for them— They consist with the fairest weather. By the mood of my mind I suddenly felt dissuaded from continuing my walk—but I observed at the same instant that the shadow of a cloud was passing one spot on which I stood— though it was of small extent—which if it had no connexion with my mood at any rate suggested how transient & little to be regarded that mood was— I kept on & In a moment the sun shone on my walk within & without.

23 July 1851, Journal *3:329–31*

❦ How far behind the spring seems now—farther off perhaps than ever—for this heat & dryness is most opposed to spring. Where most I sought for flowers in April . . . I do not think to go now—it is either drought & barrenness or fall there now. The reign of moisture is long since over— For a long time the year feels the influence of the snows of winter & the long rains of spring— But now how changed! It is like another & a fabulous age to look back on. When earth's veins were full of moisture & violets burst out on every hill-side. Spring is the reign of water— Summer of heat & dryness. Winter of cold Whole families of plants that lately flourished have disappeared. Now the phenomena are tropical. Let our summer last long enough & our land would wear the aspects of the tropics.— The luxuriant foliage & growth of all kinds shades the earth & is converting every copse into a jungle. Vegetation is rampant— There is not such rapid growth it is true, but it slumbers like a serpent that has swallowed its prey. Summer is one long drought. Rain is the exception— All the signs of it fail for it is dry weather— Though it may seem so the current year is not peculiar in this respect. It is a slight labor to keep account of all the showers[,] the rainy days of a summer— You may keep it on your thumbnail . . .

The berries of the v[accinium] vacillans are very abundant & large this year on Fair Haven where I am now— Indeed these & huckleberries and black berries are very abundant in this part of the town. Nature does her best to feed man. The traveller need not go out of the road to get as many as he wants—every bush & vine teems with palatable fruit. Man for once stands in such relation to Nature as the animals—they pluck & eat as they go. The fields & hills are a table constantly spread— Wines of all kinds & qualities of noblest vintages are bottled up in the skins of countless berries—for the taste of men & animals. To men they seem offered not so much for food as for sociality—that they may picnic with nature— Diet drinks—cordials—wines— We pluck & eat in remembrance of Her— It is a sacrament—a communion. The not forbidden fruits—which no serpent tempts us to taste. Slight & innocent savors—which relate us to nature—make us her guests & entitle us to her regard & protection—

24 July 1853, Journal *6:264–67*

❦ I THINK THAT I SPEAK impartially when I say that I have never met with a stream so suitable for boating and botanizing as the Concord, and fortunately nobody knows it. I know of reaches which a single country-seat would spoil beyond remedy, but there has not been any important change here since I can remember. The willows slumber along its shore, piled in light but low masses, even like the cumuli clouds above. We pass haymakers in every meadow, who may think that we are idlers. But Nature takes care that every nook and crevice is explored by some one. While they look after the open meadows, we farm the track between the river's brinks and behold the shores from that side. We, too, are harvesting an annual crop with our eyes, and think you Nature is not glad to display her beauty to us?

6 August 1858, Journal *XI:77*

❦ IF I WERE TO CHOOSE a time for a friend to make a passing visit to this world for the first time in the full possession of all his faculties perchance it would be at a moment when the sun was setting with splendor in the west—his light reflected far & wide through the clarified air after a rain—and a brilliant rain-bow as now o[v]erarching the eastern sky. Would he be likely to think this a vulgar place to live where one would weary of existence—and be compelled to devote his life to frivolity & dissipation? If a man travelling from world to world were to pass through this world at such a moment would he not be tempted to take up his abode here?

7 August 1852, Journal *5:287*

❦ IT IS INSPIRITING at last to hear the wind whistle & moan about my attic—after so much trivial summer weather—& to feel cool. . . .

Do you not feel the fruit of your spring & summer beginning to ripen, to harden its seed within you— Do not your thoughts begin to acquire consistency as well as flavor & ripeness— How can we expect a harvest of thought who have not had a seed-time of character— Already some of my small thoughts—fruit of my spring life—are ripe, like the berries which feed the 1st broods of birds,—and other some are prematurely ripe & bright like the lower leaves of the herbs which have felt the summer's drought—

Seasons when our mind is like the strings of a harp which is swept—& we stand and listen. A man may hear strains in his thought far surpassing any oratorio—

. . . From this off side of the year—this imbricated slope with alternating burnished surfaces & shady ledges—much more light & heat are reflected (less absorbed) methinks than from the springward side. In midsummer we are of the earth—confounded with it & covered with its dust Now we begin to erect ourselves somewhat & walk upon its surface. I am not so much reminded of former years, as of existence prior to years—

7 August 1854, Journal *8:257–58*

❦ FOR A DAY OR TWO it has been quite cool—a coolness that was felt even when sitting by an open window in a thin coat on the west side of the house in the morning—& you naturally sought the sun at that hour— The coolness concentrated your thought however— As I could not command a sunny window I went

abroad . . . and lay in the sun in the fields in my thin coat though
it was rather cool even there. I feel as if this coolness would do
me good. If it only makes my life more pensive why should pen-
siveness be akin to sadness. There is a certain fertile sadness
which I would not avoid but rather earnestly seek— It is posi-
tively joyful to me— It saves my life from being trivial. My life
flows with a deeper current—no longer as a shallow & brawling
stream parched & shrunken by the summer heats— This coolness comes to condense the dews & clear the atmosphere. The
stillness seems more deep & significant—each sound seems to
come from out a greater thoughtfulness in nature—as if nature
had acquired some character & mind—the cricket—the gurgling—stream—the rushing wind amid the trees—all speak
to me soberly yet encouragingly of the steady onward progress of the universe— My heart leaps into my mouth at the
sound of the wind in the woods— I whose life was but yesterday so desultory & shallow—suddenly recover my spirits—my
spirituality through my hearing. . . . Ah! if I could so live that
there should be no desultory moment in all my life! That in
the trivial season when small fruits are ripe my fruits might be
ripe also[;] that I could match nature always with my moods!
That in each season when some part of nature especially flourishes—then a corresponding part of me may not fail to flourish
Ah, I would walk I would sit & sleep with natural piety— . . .
I sometimes feels as if I were rewarded merely for expecting
better hours— I did not despair of worthier moods—and now I
have occasion to be grateful for the flood of life that is flowing
over me. I am not so poor— I can smell the ripening apples—
the very rills are deep—the autumnal flowers the trichostema
dichotoma—not only its bright blue flower above the sand but
its strong wormwood scent which belongs to the season feed

my spirit—endear the earth to me—make me value myself &
rejoice— The quivering of pigeons' wings—reminds me of the
tough fibre of the air which they rend. I thank you God. I do not
deserve anything . . . & yet I am made to rejoice. I am impure &
worthless—& yet the world is gilded for my delight & holidays
are prepared for me—& my path is strewn with flowers But
I cannot thank the Giver— I cannot even whisper my thanks
to those human friends I have. It seems to me that I am more
rewarded for my expectations than for anything I do or can do.
Ah I would not tread on a cricket in whose song is such a revelation—so soothing & cheering to my ear. O keep my senses
pure! And why should I speak to my friends? for how rarely is
it that I am I—and are they, then, they? We will meet then far
away. The seeds of the summer are getting dry & falling from
a thousand nodding heads. If I did not know you through thick
& thin how should I know you at all? Ah the very brooks seem
fuller of reflections than they were—ah such provoking sybil-
line sentences they are— —the shallowest is all at once unfath-
omable— how can that depth be fathomed where a man may
see himself reflected— The rill I stopped to drink at I drink in
more than I expected— I satisfy—& still provoke the thirst of
thirsts— . . . I do not drink in vain I mark that brook as if I had
swallowed a water snake—that would live in my stomach— I
have swallowed something worth the while— The [day] is not
what it was before I stooped to drink. Ah I shall hear from that
draught—it is not in vain that I have drunk.— I have drank an
arrow-head. It flows from where all fountains rise.

17 August 1851, Journal *3:367–69*

❦ WHAT A FACULTY must that be which can paint the most
barren landscape and humblest life in glorious colors It is pure
& invigorated senses reacting on a sound & strong imagination.
Is not that the poets case? The intellect of most men is barren.
They neither fertilize nor are fertilized. It is the mariage of the
soul with nature that makes the intellect fruitful—that gives
birth to imagination. When we were dead & dry as the high-way
some sense which has been healthily fed will put us in relation
with nature in sympathy with her—some grains of fertilizing
pollen floating in the air fall on us—& suddenly the sky is all
one rain bow—is full of music & fragrance & flavor— . . .

There is some advantage intellectually & spiritually in taking
wide views with the bodily eye & not pursuing an occupation
which holds the body prone— There is some advantage perhaps in attending to the general features of the landscape over
studying the particular plants & animals which inhabit it. A
man may walk abroad & no more see the sky than if he walked
under a shed. The poet is more in the air than the naturalist
though they may walk side by side.— Granted that you are out
of door—but what if the outer door *is* open, if the inner door
is shut. You must walk sometimes perfectly free—not prying
nor inquisitive—not bent upon seeing things— Throw away
a whole day for a single expansion[,] a single inspiration of
air—

21 August 1851, Journal *4:3–6*

❦ POKE STEMS are now ripe. I walked through a beautiful grove
of them, six or seven feet high, on the side of Lee's Cliff, where
they have ripened early. Their stems are a deep, rich purple with
a bloom, contrasting with the clear green leaves. Every part but

the leaves is a brilliant purple . . . or, more strictly speaking, the racemes without the berries are a brilliant lake-red with crimson flame-like reflections. . . . Its cylindrical racemes of berries of various hues from green to dark purple, six or seven inches long, are drooping on all sides, beautiful both with and without berries, all afire with ripeness. Its stalks, thus full of purple wine, are one of the fruits of autumn. It excites me to behold it. What a success [it is]! What maturity it arrives [at], ripening from leaf to root! May I mature as perfectly, root and branch, as the poke! Its stems are more beautiful than most flowers. It is the emblem of a successful life, a not premature death,—whose death is an ornament to nature. To walk amid these upright branching casks of purple wine, which retain and diffuse a sunset glow, for nature's vintage is not confined to the vine! I drink it with my eyes. Our poets have sung wine, the product of a foreign plant which they never saw, as if our own plants had no juice in them more than our poets. Here are berries enough to paint the western sky with and play the Bacchanal if you will. What flutes its ensanguined stems would make, to be used in the dance! It is a royal plant. I could spend the evening of the year musing amid the poke stems!

Live in each season as it passes; breathe the air, drink the drink, taste the fruit, and resign yourself to the influences of each. Let them be your only diet drink and botanical medicines. In August live on berries, not dried meats and pemmican, as if you were on shipboard making your way through a waste ocean, or in a northern desert. Be blown on by all the winds. Open your pores and bathe in all the tides of Nature, in all her streams and oceans, at all seasons. Miasma and infection are from within, not without. The invalid, brought to the brink of the grave by an unnatural life, instead of imbibing only the great influence that Nature is, drinks only the tea made of a particular herb, while he still continues his unnatural life,—saves at the spile and wastes at the bung. He does not love Nature or his life, and so sickens and dies, and no doctor can cure him. Grow green with spring, yellow and ripe with autumn. Drink of each season's influence as a vial, a true panacea of all remedies mixed for your especial use. The vials of summer never made a man sick, but those which he stored in his cellar. Drink the wines, not of your bottling, but of Nature's bottling; not kept in goat-skins or pig-skins, but the skins of a myriad fair berries. Let Nature do your bottling and your pickling and preserving. For all Nature is doing her best each moment to make us well. She exists for no other end. Do not resist her. With the least inclination to be well, we should not be sick. Men have discovered—or they think they have discovered—the salutariness of a few wild things only, and not of all nature. Why, "nature" is but another name for health, and the seasons are but different states of health. Some men think that they are not well in spring, or summer, or autumn, or winter; it is only because they are not *well in* them.

23 August 1853, Journal *V:393–95*

❦ THINK WHAT A REFUGE there is for me before August is over, from college commencements and society that isolates me! I can skulk amid the tufts of purple wood grass on the borders of the Great Fields! Wherever I walk this afternoon the purple-fringed grass stands like a guide-board and points my thoughts to more poetic paths than they have lately travelled.

A man shall, perchance, rush by and trample down plants as high as his head, and cannot be said to know that they exist, though he may have cut and cured many tons of them for his cattle. Yet, perchance, if he ever favorably attend to them, he may be overcome by their beauty.

Each humblest plant, or weed, as we call it, stands there to express some thought or mood of ours, and yet how long it stands in vain! I have walked these Great Fields so many Augusts and never yet distinctly recognized these purple companions that I have there. I have brushed against them and trampled them down, forsooth, and now at last they have, as it were, risen up and blessed me. Beauty and true wealth are always thus cheap and despised. Heaven, or paradise, might be defined as the place which men avoid. Who can doubt that these grasses which the farmer says are of no account to him find some compensation in my appreciation of them? I may say that I never saw them before, or can only recall a dim vision of them, and now wherever I go I hardly see anything else. It is the reign and presidency only of the andropogons.

26 August 1858, Journal *XI:126–27*

❧ JUNE, JULY, AND AUGUST, the tortoise eggs are hatching a few inches beneath the surface in sandy fields. You tell of active labors, of works of art, and wars the past summer; meanwhile the tortoise eggs underlie this turmoil. . . . June, July, and August,—the livelong summer,—what are they with their heats and fevers but sufficient to hatch a tortoise in. Be not in haste; mind your private affairs. Consider the turtle. A whole summer—June, July, and August—is not too good nor too much to hatch a turtle in. Perchance you have worried yourself, despaired of the world, meditated the end of life, and all things seemed rushing to destruction; but nature has steadily and serenely advanced with a turtle's pace. The young turtle spends its infancy within its shell. It gets experience and learns the ways of the world through that wall. While it rests warily on the edge of its hole, rash schemes are undertaken by men and fail. Has not the tortoise also learned the true value of time? You go to India and back, and the turtle eggs in your field are still unhatched. French empires rise or fall, but the turtle is developed only so fast. What's a summer? Time for a turtle's eggs to hatch. So is the turtle developed, fitted to endure, for he outlives twenty French dynasties. One turtle knows several Napoleons. They have seen no berries, had no cares, yet has not the great world existed for them as much as for you?

28 August 1856, Journal *IX:32–33*

❦ BOTH A CONSCIOUS and an unconscious life are good. Neither is good exclusively, for both have the same source. The wisely conscious life springs out of an unconscious suggestion. I have found my account in travelling in having prepared beforehand a list of questions which I would get answered, not trusting to my interest at the moment, and can then travel with the most profit. Indeed, it is by obeying the suggestions of a higher light within you that you escape from yourself and, in the transit, as it were see with the unworn sides of your eyes, travel totally new paths. What is that pretended life that does not take up a claim, that does not occupy ground, that cannot build a causeway to its objects, that sits on a bank looking over a bog, singing its desires?

. . . It is in vain to dream of a wildness distant from ourselves. There is none such. . . . I shall never find in the wilds of Labrador any greater wildness than in some recess in Concord, *i.e.* than I import into it. A little more manhood or virtue will make the surface of the globe anywhere thrillingly novel and wild. That alone will provide and pay the fiddler; it will convert the district road into an untrodden cranberry bog, for it restores all things to their original primitive flourishing and promising state.

30 August 1856, Journal *IX:37–38, 43*

❦ MOONLIGHT ON FAIR HAVEN POND seen from the Cliffs. A sheeny lake in the midst of a boundless forest— The windy surf sounding freshly & wildly in the single pine behind you— The silence of hushed wolves in the wilderness & as you fancy moose looking off from the shore of the lake. The stars of poetry & history—& unexplored nature looking down on the scene. This is my world now—with a dull whitish mark curving northward through the forest marking the outlet to the lake. Fair Haven by moonlight lies there like a lake in the Maine Wilderness in the midst of a primitive forest untrodden by man. This light & this hour takes the civilization all out of the landscape— Even in villages dogs bay the moon, in forests like this we listen to hear wolves howl to Cynthia.

5 September 1851, Journal *4:47*

❦ OUR EXTATIC STATES which appear to yield so little fruit, have this value at least—though in the seasons when our genius reigns we may be powerless for expression.— Yet in calmer seasons, when our talent is active, the memory of those rarer moods comes to color our picture & is the permanent paint pot as it were into which we dip our brush

Thus no life or experience goes unreported at last—but if it be not solid gold it is gold-leaf which gilds the furniture of the mind. It is an experience of infinite beauty—on which we unfailing draw. Which enables us to exaggerate ever truly. Our moments of inspiration are not lost though we have no particular poems to show for them. For those experiences have left an indelible impression, and we are ever and anon reminded of them. . . .

Suppose you attend to the hints to the suggestions which the moon makes for one month . . . will they not be very diffirent from any thing in literature or religion or philosophy. The scenery, when it is truly seen reacts on the life of the seer. How to live— How to get the most life! . . . How to extract its honey from the flower of the world. That is my every day business. I am as busy as a bee about it. I ramble over all fields on that errand and am never so happy as when I feel myself heavy with honey & wax. I am like a bee searching the livelong day for the sweets of nature. . . . I do so as naturally & as joyfully with my own humming music—seek honey all the day. With what honied thought any experience yields me I take a bee line to my cell. It is with flowers I would deal. Where is the flower there is the honey—which is perchance the nectareous portion of the fruit—there is to be the fruit—& no doubt flowers are thus colored & painted—to attract & guide the bee. So by the dawning or radiance of beauty are we advertised where is the honey & the fruit of thought of discourse & of action— We are first attracted by the beauty of the flower, before we discover the honey which is a foretaste of the future fruit. . . .

My profession is to be always on the alert to find God in nature—to know his lurking places. To attend all the oratorios—the operas in nature.

7 *September 1851*, Journal *4:51–55*

❦ Do not the song of birds & the fireflies go with the grass?
While the grass is fresh the earth is in its vigor. The greenness of the grass is the best symptom or evidence of the earth's
youth or health. . . . Perhaps a history of the year would be a
history of the grass—or of a leaf regarding the grass blades
as leaves—for it is equally true that the leaves soon loose
their freshness & soundness, & become the prey of insects &
of drought. Plants commonly soon cease to grow for the year
unless they may have a fall growth—which is a kind of 2nd
spring. In the feelings of the man too the year is already past
& he looks forward to the coming winter. His occasional reju-
venescence & faith in the current time is like the aftermath⦂
a scanty crop. The enterprise which he has not already undertaken—cannot be undertaken this year. The period of youth is
past. The year may be in its summer—in its manhood, but it is
no longer in the flower of its age— It is a season of withering
of dust & heat—a season of small fruits & trivial experiences.
Summer thus answers to manhood. But there is an aftermath
in early autumn—& some spring flowers bloom again—fol-
lowed by an Indian summer of finer atmosphere & of a pensive
beauty. May my life be not destitute of its Indian summer— A
season of fine & clear mild weather when I may prolong my
hunting before the winter comes. When I may once more lie on
the ground with faith as in spring—& even with more serene
confidence—

8 September 1851, Journal *4:62–63*

❦ THINKING THIS AFTERNOON of the prospect of my writing
lectures and going abroad to read them the next winter, I realized how incomparably great the advantages of obscurity and
poverty which I have enjoyed so long (and may still perhaps
enjoy). I thought with what more than princely, with what
poetical, leisure I had spent my years hitherto, without care or
engagement, fancy-free. I have given myself up to nature; I have
lived so many springs and summers and autumns and winters
as if I had nothing else to do but *live* them, and imbibe whatever
nutriment they had for me; I have spent a couple of years, for
instance, with the flowers chiefly, having none other so bind-
ing engagement as to observe when they opened; I could have
afforded to spend a whole fall observing the changing tints of
the foliage. Ah, how I have thriven on solitude and poverty! I
cannot overstate this advantage. . . .

It has been my vacation, my season of growth and expansion,
a prolonged youth.

19 September 1854, Journal *VII:46*

❦ IT IS A LUXURY to muse by a wall-side in the sunshine of a
September afternoon—to cuddle down under a gray stone, and
harken to the siren song of the cricket. Day and night seem
henceforth but accidents—and the time is always a still even
tide, and as the close of a happy day.— Parched fields and mul-
leins gilded with the slanting rays are my diet.— I know of
no word so fit to express this disposition of nature as—Alma-
Natura.

20 September 1838, Journal *1:56*

AUTUMN

CELTIS BERRIES BEGIN to yellow. As I look off from the hilltop, I wonder if there are any finer days in the year than these. The air is so fine and more bracing, and the landscape has acquired some fresh verdure withal. The frosts come to ripen the year, the days, like fruits,—persimmons.

What if we were to walk by sunlight with equal abstraction and aloofness, yet with equally impartial observation and criticism. As if it shone not for you, nor you for it, but you had come forth into it for the nonce to admire it. By moonlight we are not of the earth earthy, but we are of the earth spiritual. So might we walk by sunlight, seeing the sun but as a moon, a comparatively faint and reflected light, and the day as a brooding night, in which we glimpse some stars still. . . .

Crossing the hill behind Minott's just as the sun is preparing to dip below the horizon, the thin haze in the atmosphere north and south along the west horizon reflects a purple tinge and bathes the mountains with the same, like a bloom on fruits. I wonder if this phenomenon is observed in warm weather, or before the frosts have come. Is it not another evidence of the ripe days? . . .

By moonlight all is simple. We are enabled to erect ourselves, our minds, on account of the fewness of objects. We are no longer distracted. It is simple as bread and water. It is simple as the rudiments of an art,—a lesson to be taken before sunlight, perchance, to prepare us for that.

22 September 1854, Journal *VII:50–51*

❧ SMALL RED MAPLES in low ground have fairly begun to burn for a week. It varies from scarlet to crimson. It looks like training-day in the meadows and swamps. They have run up their colors. A small red maple has grown, perchance, far away on some moist hillside, a mile from any road, unobserved. It has faithfully discharged the duties of a maple there, all winter and summer, neglected none of its economies, added to its stature in the virtue which belongs to a maple, by a steady growth all summer, and is nearer heaven than in the spring, never having gone gadding abroad; and now, in this month of September, when men are turned travellers, hastening to the seaside, or the mountains, or the lakes,—in this month of travelling,—this modest maple, having ripened its seeds, still without budging an inch, travels on its reputation, runs up its scarlet flag on that hillside, to show that it has finished its summer work before all other trees, and withdraws from the contest. Thus that modest worth which no scrutiny could have detected when it was most industrious, is, by the very tint of its maturity, by its very blushes, revealed at last to the most careless and distant observer. It rejoices in its existence; its reflections are unalloyed. . . . In its hue is no regret nor pining. Its leaves have been asking their parent from time to time in a whisper, "When shall we redden?" It has faithfully husbanded its sap, and builded without babbling nearer and nearer to heaven. Long since it committed its seeds to the winds and has the satisfaction of knowing perhaps that a thousand little well-behaved and promising maples of its stock are already established in business somewhere. It deserves well of Mapledom. It has afforded a shelter to the wandering bird. Its autumnal tint shows how it has spent its summer; it is the hue of its virtue.

27 September 1857, Journal *X:46–48*

❧ How interesting now, by wall-sides and on open springy hillsides, the large, straggling tufts of the dicksonia fern above the leaf-strewn greensward, the cold fall-green sward! They are unusually preserved about the Corner Spring, considering the earliness of this year. Long, handsome lanceolate green fronds, pointing in every direction, recurved and full of fruit, intermixed with yellowish and sere brown and shrivelled ones. The whole clump, perchance, strewn with fallen and withered maple leaves and overtopped by now withered and unnoticed osmundas. Their lingering greenness so much the more noticeable now that the leaves (generally) have changed. They affect us as if they were evergreen, such persistent life and greenness in the midst of their own decay. I do not notice them so much in summer. No matter how much withered they are, with withered leaves that have fallen on them, moist and green they spire above them, not fearing the frosts, fragile as they are. Their greenness so much the more interesting because so many have already fallen and we know that the first severer frost will cut off them too. In the summer greenness is cheap; now it is something comparatively rare and is the emblem of life to us.

4 October 1859, Journal *XII:370–71*

❦ THE VISITATIONS OF GENIUS are unbribed as the dawn. It is by patient and unanxious labor at the anvil that fairer mornings are to be compelled.

A part of me which has reposed in silence all day, goes abroad at night, like the owl, and has its day.

At night we recline, and nestle, and infold ourselves in our being. Each night I go home to rest. Each night I am gathered to my fathers. The soul departs out of the body, and sleeps in God, a divine slumber. As she withdraws herself, the limbs droop and the eyelids fall, and nature reclaims her clay again. Men have always regarded the night as ambrosial or divine. The air is then peopled—fairies come out.

5 October 1840, Journal *1:184*

❦ AS I SAT ON THE HIGH BANK at the east end of Walden this afternoon, at five o'clock, I saw, by a peculiar intention or dividing of the eye, a very striking subaqueous rainbow-like phenomenon. A passer-by might, perhaps would, have noticed that the bright-tinted shrubs about the high shore in the sunny side were reflected in the water; but, unless on the alert for such effects, he would have failed to perceive the full beauty of the phenomenon. Unless you look for reflections, you commonly will not find them. Those brilliant shrubs, which were from three to a dozen feet in height, were all reflected, dimly so far as the details of leaves, etc., were concerned, but brightly as to color, and, of course, in the order in which they stood,—scarlet, yellow, green, etc.; but, there being a slight ripple on the surface, these reflections were not true to their height though true to their breadth, but were extended downward with mathematical perpendicularity, three or four times too far, forming sharp pyramids of the several colors, gradually reduced to mere dusky points. The effect of this prolongation of the reflection was a very pleasing softening and blending of the colors, especially when a small bush of one bright tint stood directly before another of a contrary and equally bright tint. It was just as if you were to brush firmly aside with your hand or a brush a fresh line of paint of various colors, or so many lumps of friable colored powders. There was, accordingly, a sort of belt, as wide as the whole height of the hill, extending downward along the whole north or sunny side of the pond, composed of exceedingly short and narrow inverted pyramids of the most brilliant colors intermixed. I have seen, indeed, similar inverted pyramids in the old drawings of tattooing about the waists of the aborigines of this country. Walden, too, like an Indian maiden, wears this broad rainbow-like belt of brilliant-colored points or cones round her waist in October. The color seems to be reflected and re-reflected from ripple to ripple, losing brightness each time by the softest possible gradation, and tapering toward the beholder, since he occupies a mere point of view. This is one of the prettiest effects of the autumnal change.

7 October 1857, Journal *X:74–76*

♥ ON LEE'S HILL-SIDE by the pond the old leaves of some pitch pines are almost of a golden Yellow hue seen in the sun light—a rich autumnal look. The green are as it were set in the yellow. The witch hazel here is in full blossom—on this magical hill-side—while its broad yellow leaves are falling—some bushes are completely bare of leaves, and leather-colored they strew the ground. It is an extremely interesting plant—October & November's child—and yet reminds me of the very earliest spring— Its blossoms smell like the spring—like the willow catkins—by their color as well as fragrance they belong to the saffron dawn of the year.— Suggesting amid all these signs of Autumn—falling leaves & frost—that the life of nature—by which she eternally flourishes, is untouched. It stands here in the shadow on the side of the hill while the sun-light from over the top of the hill lights up its topmost sprays & yellow blossoms. Its spray so jointed and angular is not to be mistaken for any other. I lie on my back with joy under its boughs. While its leaves fall—its blossoms spring. The autumn then is in deed a spring. All the year is a spring. I see two blackbirds high over head going south, but I am going north in my thought with these hazel blossoms . . .

It is a faery-place. This is a part of the immortality of the soul.

9 October 1851, Journal *4:135–36*

🌷 TALK ABOUT LEARNING our *letters* and being *literate!* Why, the roots of *letters* are *things.* Natural objects and phenomena are the original symbols or types which express our thoughts and feelings, and yet American scholars, having little or no root in the soil, commonly strive with all their might to confine themselves to the imported symbols alone. All the true growth and experience, the living speech, they would fain reject. . . . It is the old error, which the church, the state, the school ever commit, choosing darkness rather than light, holding fast to the old and to tradition. A more intimate knowledge, a deeper experience, will surely originate a word. When I really know that our river pursues a serpentine course to the Merrimack, shall I continue to describe it by referring to some other river no older than itself which is like it, and call it a *meander?* It is no more *meandering* than the Meander is *musketaquidding.* As well sing of the nightingale here as the Meander. What if there were a tariff on words, on language, for the encouragement of home manufactures? Have we not the genius to coin our own? Let the schoolmaster distinguish the true from the counterfeit.

They go on publishing the "chronological cycles" and "movable festivals of the Church" and the like from mere habit, but how insignificant are these compared with the annual phenomena of your life, which fall within your experience! The signs of the zodiac are not nearly of that significance to me that the sight of a dead sucker in the spring is. That is the occasion for an *im*movable festival in my church. Another kind of Lent then begins in my thoughts than you wot of. . . .

Men attach a false importance to celestial phenomena as compared with terrestrial, as if it were more respectable and elevating to watch your neighbors than to mind your own affairs. The nodes of the stars are not the knots we have to untie. The phenomena of our year are one thing, those of the almanac another. For October, for instance, instead of making the sun enter the sign of the scorpion, I would much sooner make him enter a musquash-house. . . . The snapping turtle, too, must find a place among the constellations, though it may have to supplant some doubtful characters already there. If there is no place for him overhead, he can serve us bravely underneath, supporting the earth.

This clear, cold, Novemberish light is inspiriting. Some twigs which are bare and weeds begin to glitter with hoary light. The very edge or outline of a tawny or russet hill has this hoary light on it. Your thoughts sparkle like the water surface and the downy twigs.

16 October 1859, Journal *XII:389–91*

❦ How pleasant to walk over beds of these fresh, crisp, and rustling fallen leaves,—young hyson, green tea, clean, crisp, and wholesome! How beautiful they go to their graves! how gently lay themselves down and turn to mould!—painted of a thousand hues and fit to make the beds of us living. So they troop to their graves, light and frisky. They put on no weeds. Merrily they go scampering over the earth, selecting their graves, whispering all through the woods about it. They that waved so loftily, how contentedly they return to dust again and are laid low, resigned to lie and decay at the foot of the tree and afford nourishment to new generations of their kind, as well as to flutter on high! How they are mixed up, all species,—oak and maple and chestnut and birch! They are about to add a leaf's breadth to the depth of the soil. We are all the richer for their decay. Nature is not cluttered with them. She is a perfect husbandman; she stores them all.

20 October 1853, Journal *V:441*

❦ The brilliant autumnal colors are red and yellow and the various tints, hues, and shades of these. Blue is reserved to be the color of the sky, but yellow and red are the colors of the earth flower. Every fruit, on ripening, and just before its fall, acquires a bright tint. So do the leaves; so the sky before the end of the day, and the year near its setting. October is the red sunset sky, November the later twilight. Color stands for all ripeness and success. We have dreamed that the hero should carry his color aloft, as a symbol of the ripeness of his virtue. The noblest feature, the eye, is the fairest-colored, the jewel of the body. The warrior's flag is the flower which precedes his fruit. He unfurls his flag to the breeze with such confidence and brag as the flower its petals. Now we shall see what kind of fruit will succeed.

The very forest and herbage, the pellicle of the earth as it were, must acquire a bright color, an evidence of its ripeness, as if the globe itself were a fruit on its stem, with ever one cheek toward the sun.

Our appetites have commonly confined our views of ripeness and its phenomena—color and mellowness and perfectness—to the fruits which we eat, and we are wont to forget that an immense harvest which we do not eat, hardly use at all, is annually ripened by nature. . . . [R]ound about and within our towns there is annually another show of fruits, on an infinitely grander scale, fruits which address our taste for beauty alone.

The scarlet oak, which was quite green on the 12th, is now completely scarlet and apparently has been so a few days. . . . Look at one, completely changed from green to bright dark-scarlet, every leaf, as if it had been dipped into a scarlet dye, between you and the sun. Was not this worth waiting for? . . .

Now in huckleberry pastures you see only here and there a few bright scarlet or crimson (for they vary) leaves amid or above the bare reddish stems, burning as if with condensed brightness,—as if the few that remained burned with the condensed brightness of all that have fallen. In sheltered woods you [see] some dicksonia still straw-color or pale-yellow. Some thoroughwort the same color. In the shade generally you find paler and more delicate tints, fading to a straw-color and white. The deep reds and scarlets and purples show exposure to the sun. I see an intensely scarlet high blueberry—but where one leaf has overlapped another it is yellow—with a regular outline.

24 October 1858, Journal *XI:243–45*

❧ THESE REGULAR PHENOMENA of the seasons get at last to be—they were *at first*, of course—simply and plainly phenomena or phases of my life. The seasons and all their changes are in me. I see not a dead eel or floating snake, or a gull, but it rounds my life and is like a line or accent in its poem. Almost I believe the Concord would not rise and overflow its banks again, were I not here. After a while I learn what my moods and seasons are. I would have nothing subtracted. I can imagine nothing added. My moods are thus periodical, not two days in my year alike. The perfect correspondence of Nature to man, so that he is at home in her! . . .

Those sparrows, too, are thoughts I have. They come and go; they flit by quickly on their migrations, uttering only a faint *chip*, I know not whither or why exactly. One will not rest upon its twig for me to scrutinize it. The whole copse will be alive with my rambling thoughts, bewildering me by their very multitude, but they will be all gone directly without leaving me a feather. My loftiest thought is somewhat like an eagle that suddenly comes into the field of view, suggesting great things and thrilling the beholder, as if it were bound hitherward with a message for me; but it comes no nearer, but circles and soars away, growing dimmer, disappointing me, till it is lost behind a cliff or a cloud.

26 October 1857, Journal *X:127–29*

❦ I TRY ONE OF THE WILD APPLES in my desk. It is remarkable that the wild apples which I praise as so spirited and racy when eaten in the fields and woods, when brought into the house have a harsh and crabbed taste. As shells and pebbles must be beheld on the seashore, so these October fruits must be tasted in a bracing walk amid the somewhat bracing airs of late October. To appreciate their wild and sharp flavors, it seems necessary that you be breathing the sharp October or November air. The outdoor air and exercise which the walker gets give a different tone to his palate, and he craves a fruit which the sedentary would call harsh and crabbed even. The palate rejects a wild apple eaten in the house—so of haws and acorns—and demands a tamed one, for here you miss that October air which is the wine it is eaten with. I frequently pluck wild apples of so rich and spicy a flavor that I wonder all orchardists do not get a scion from them, but when I have brought home my pockets full, and taste them in the house, they are unexpectedly harsh, crude things. They must be eaten in the fields, when your system is all aglow with exercise, the frosty weather nips your fingers (in November), the wind rattles the bare boughs and rustles the leaves, and the jay is heard screaming around.

So there is one thought for the field, another for the house. I would have my thoughts, like wild apples, to be food for walkers, and will not warrant them to be palatable if tasted in the house.

To appreciate the flavor of those wild apples requires vigorous and healthy senses, papillæ firm and erect on the tongue and palate, not easily tamed and flattened. Some of those apples might be labelled, "To be eaten in the wind."

27 October 1855, Journal *VII:520–21*

❧ IN THE LEE FARM SWAMP, by the old Sam Barrett mill site, I see two kinds of ferns still green and much in fruit. . . . In the summer you might not have noticed them. Now they are conspicuous amid the withered leaves. . . . What means this persistent vitality, invulnerable to frost and wet? Why were these spared when the brakes and osmundas were stricken down? They stay as if to keep up the spirits of the cold-blooded frogs which have not yet gone into the mud; that the summer may die with decent and graceful moderation, gradually. Is not the water of the spring improved by their presence? They fall back and droop here and there, like the plumes of departing summer,—of the departing year. Even in them I feel an argument for immortality. Death is so far from being universal. The same destroyer does not destroy all. How valuable they are . . . for cheerfulness. Greenness at the end of the year, after the fall of the leaf, as in a hale old age. To my eyes they are tall and noble as palm groves, and always some forest nobleness seems to have its haunt under their umbrage. Each such green tuft of ferns is a grove where some nobility dwells and walks. All that was immortal in the swamp's herbage seems here crowded into smaller compass,—the concentrated greenness of the swamp. How dear they must be to the chickadee and the rabbit! The cool, slowly retreating rear-guard of the swamp army. What virtue is theirs that enables them to resist the frost?

If you are afflicted with melancholy at this season, go to the swamp and see the brave spears of skunk-cabbage buds already advanced toward a new year. Their gravestones are not bespoken yet. . . . "Up and at 'em," "Give it to 'em," "Excelsior," "Put it through,"—these are their mottoes. Mortal human creatures must take a little respite in this fall of the year; their spirits do flag a little. There is a little questioning of destiny, and thinking to go like cowards to where the "weary shall be at rest." But not so with the skunk-cabbage. Its withered leaves fall and are transfixed by a rising bud. Winter and death are ignored; the circle of life is complete. Are these false prophets? Is it a lie or a vain boast underneath the skunk-cabbage bud, pushing it upward and lifting the dead leaves with it? They rest with spears advanced; they rest to shoot!

I say it is good for me to be here, slumping in the mud, a trap covered with withered leaves. See those green cabbage buds lifting the dry leaves in that watery and muddy place. There is no can't nor cant to them. They see over the brow of winter's hill. They see another summer ahead.

31 October 1857, Journal *X:149–51*

❦ As the afternoons grow shorter, and the early evening drives us home to complete our chores, we are reminded of the shortness of life, and become more pensive, at least in this twilight of the year. We are prompted to make haste and finish our work before the night comes. I leaned over a rail in the twilight on the Walden road, waiting for the evening mail to be distributed, when such thoughts visited me. I seemed to recognize the November evening as a familiar thing come round again, and yet I could hardly tell whether I had ever known it or only divined it. The November twilights just begun! It appeared like a part of a panorama at which I sat spectator, a part with which I was perfectly familiar just coming into view, and I foresaw how it would look and roll along, and prepared to be pleased. Just such a piece of art merely, though infinitely sweet and grand, did it appear to me, and just as little were any active duties required of me. We are independent o[f] all that we see. The hangman whom I have *seen* cannot hang me. The earth which I have *seen* cannot bury me. Such doubleness and distance does sight prove. Only the rich and such as are troubled with ennui are implicated in the maze of phenomena. You cannot see anything until you are clear of it. The long railroad causeway through the meadows west of me, the still twilight in which hardly a cricket was heard, the dark bank of clouds in the horizon long after sunset, the villagers crowding the post-office, and the hastening home to supper by candle-light, had I not seen all this before! What new sweet was I to extract from it? Truly they mean that we shall learn our lesson well. Nature gets thumbed like an old spelling-book. The almshouse and Frederick were still as last November. I was no nearer, methinks, nor further off from my friends. Yet I sat the bench with perfect contentment, unwilling to exchange the familiar vision that was to be unrolled for any treasure or heaven that could be imagined. . . . It was as if I was promised the greatest novelty the world has ever seen or shall see, though the utmost possible novelty would be the difference between me and myself a year ago. This alone encouraged me, and was my fuel for the approaching winter. That we may behold the panorama with this slight improvement or change, this is what we sustain life for with so much effort from year to year.

And yet there is no more tempting novelty than this new November. No going to Europe or another world is to be named with it. Give me the old familiar walk, post-office and all, with this ever new self, with this infinite expectation and faith, which does not know when it is beaten. We'll go nutting once more. We'll pluck the nut of the world, and crack it in the winter evenings. Theatres and all other sightseeing are puppet-shows in comparison. I will take another walk to the Cliff, another row on the river, another skate on the meadow, be out in the first snow, and associate with the winter birds. Here I am at home. In the bare and bleached crust of the earth I recognize my friend.

1 November 1858, Journal *XI:273–75*

❦ I THINK THAT MOST MEN, as farmers, hunters, fishers, etc., walk along a river's bank, or paddle along its stream, without seeing the reflections. Their minds are not abstracted from the surface, from surfaces generally. It is only a reflecting mind that sees reflections. I am often aware that I have been occupied with shallow and commonplace thoughts, looking for something superficial, when I did not see the most glorious reflections, though exactly in the line of my vision. If the fisherman was looking at the reflection, he would not know when he had a nibble! I know from my own experience that he may cast his line right over the most elysian landscape and sky, and not *catch* the slightest notion of them. You must be in an abstract mood to see reflections however distinct. I was even startled by the sight of that reflected red oak as if it were a water-spirit. When we are enough abstracted, the opaque earth itself reflects images to us; *i.e.*, we are imaginative, see visions, etc. Such a reflection, this inky, leafy tree, against the white sky, can only be seen at this season.

2 November 1857, Journal *X:156–57*

❦ As I RETURN DOWN the Boulder Field, I see the now winter-colored—*i.e.* reddish (of oak leaves)—horizon of hills, with its few white houses, four or five miles distant southward, between two of the boulders, which are a dozen rods from me, a dozen feet high, and nearly as much apart,—as a landscape between the frame of a picture. But what a picture-frame! These two great slumbering masses of rock, reposing like a pair of mastodons on the surface of the pasture, completely shutting out a mile of the horizon on each side, while between their adjacent sides, which are nearly perpendicular, I see the now purified, dry, reddish, leafy horizon, with a faint tinge of blue from the distance. To see a remote landscape between two near rocks! I want no other gilding to my picture-frame. There they lie, as perchance they tumbled and split from off an iceberg. What better frame could you have? The globe itself, here named pasture, for ground and foreground, two great boulders for the sides of the frame, and the sky itself for the top! And for artists and subject, God and Nature! Such pictures cost nothing but eyes, and it will not bankrupt one to own them. . . . [N]one can doubt but they are really the works of an old master.

3 November 1857, Journal *X:158-59*

❦ I AM STRUCK by the fact that the more slowly trees grow at first, the sounder they are at the core, and I think the same is true of human beings. We do not wish to see children precocious, making great strides in their early years like sprouts, producing a soft and perishable timber, but better if they expand slowly at first, as if contending with difficulties, and so are solidified and perfected. Such trees continue to expand with nearly equal rapidity to an extreme old age.

5 November 1860, Journal *XIV:217*

❧ CLIMBED THE WOODED HILL by Holden's spruce swamp and got a novel view of the river and Fair Haven Bay through the almost leafless woods. How much handsomer a river or lake such as ours, seen thus through a foreground of scattered or else partially leafless trees, though at a considerable distance this side of it, especially if the water is open, without wooded shores or isles! It is the most perfect and beautiful of all frames, which yet the sketcher is commonly careful to brush aside. I mean a pretty thick foreground, a view of the distant water through the near forest, through a thousand little vistas, as we are rushing toward the former,—that intimate mingling of wood and water which excites an expectation which the near and open view rarely realizes. We prefer that some part be concealed, which our imagination may navigate.

6 November 1853, Journal *V:480–81*

❧ I FIND IT GOOD to be out this still, dark, mizzling afternoon; my walk or voyage is more suggestive and profitable than in bright weather. The view is contracted by the misty rain, the water is perfectly smooth, and the stillness is favorable to reflection. I am more open to impressions, more sensitive (not

calloused or indurated by sun and wind), as if in a chamber still.
My thoughts are concentrated; I am all compact. The solitude
is real, too, for the weather keeps other men at home. This mist
is like a roof and walls over and around, and I walk with a
domestic feeling. The sound of a wagon going over an unseen
bridge is louder than ever, and so of other sounds. I am *compelled* to look at near objects. All things have a soothing effect;
the very clouds and mists brood over me. My power of observation and contemplation is much increased. My attention does
not wander. The world and my life are simplified. What now of
Europe and Asia?

7 November 1855, Journal *VIII:14*

❦ As I stood upon Heywood's Peak, I observed in the very
middle of the pond, which was smooth and reflected the sky
there, what at first I took to be a sheet of very thin, dark ice two
yards wide drifting there, the first ice of the season, which had
formed by the shore in the morning, but immediately I considered that it was too early and warm for that. Then I wondered
for a moment what dark film could be floating out there on the
pure and unruffled lake. To be sure, it was not a very conspicuous object, and most would not have noticed it! But, suspecting
what it was, I looked through my glass and could plainly see the
dimples made by a school of little fishes continually coming to
the surface there together. It was exactly analogous to the dark
rippled patches on the sea made by the menhaden as seen from
Cape Cod. Why have I never observed the like in the river? In
this respect . . . Walden is a small ocean.

We had a true November sunset after a dark, cloudy afternoon. The sun reached a clear stratum just before setting, beneath the dark cloud, though ready to enter another on the horizon's edge, and a cold, yellow sunlight suddenly illumined the withered grass of the fields around, near and far, eastward. Such a phenomenon as, when it occurs later, I call the afterglow of the year.

9 November 1858, Journal *XI:303–4*

❦ ONE MUST needs climb a hill to know what a world he inhabits. In the midst of this Indian summer I am perched on the topmost rock of Nawshawtuct—a velvet wind blowing from the south west— I seem to feel the atoms as they strike my cheek. Hills, mountains, steeples stand out in bold relief in the horizon—while I am resting on the rounded boss of an enormous shield—the river like a vein of silver encircling its edge—and thence the shield gradually rises to its rim the horizon. Not a cloud is to be seen, but villages—villas—forests—mountains—one above another, till they are swallowed up in the heavens. The atmosphere is such that as I look abroad upon the length and breadth of the land—it recedes from my eye, and I seem to be looking for the threads of the velvet.

Thus I admire the grandeur of my emerald carriage—with its border of blue—in which I am rolling through space.

21 November 1837, Journal *1:14*

❦ THIS IS NOVEMBER of the hardest kind,—bare frozen ground covered with pale-brown or straw-colored herbage, a strong, cold, cutting northwest wind which makes me seek to cover my ears, a perfectly clear and cloudless day. The cattle in the fields have a cold, shrunken, shaggy look, their hair hanging out every way, as if with electricity, like the cat's. Ditches and pools are fast skimming over, and a few slate-colored snow-birds, with thick, shuffling twitter, and fine-chipping tree sparrows flit from bush to bush in the otherwise deserted pastures. This month taxes a walker's resources more than any. For my part, I should sooner think of going into quarters in November than in the winter. If you do feel any fire at this season out of doors, you may depend upon it, it is your own. It is but a short time, these afternoons, before the night cometh, in which no man can walk. . . . November Eat-heart,—is that the name of it? Not only the fingers cease to do their office, but there is often a benumbing of the faculties generally. You can hardly screw up your courage to take a walk when all is thus tightly locked or frozen up and so little is to be seen in field or wood. I am inclined to take to the swamps or woods as the warmest place, and the former are still the openest. Nature has herself become like the few fruits which she still affords, a very thick-shelled nut with a shrunken meat within. If I find anything to excite or warm my thoughts abroad, it is an agreeable disappointment, for I am obliged to go abroad willfully and against my inclinations at first. The prospect looks so barren, so many springs are frozen up, not a flower perchance and but few birds left, not a companion abroad in all these fields for me, I am slow to go forth. I seem to anticipate a fruitless walk. . . . But then I am often unexpectedly compensated, and the thinnest yellow light of November is more warming and exhilarating than any wine they tell of; and then the mite which November contributes becomes equal in value to the bounty of July. I may meet with something which interests me, and immediately it is as warm as in July, as if it were the south instead of the northwest wind that blowed.

25 November 1857, Journal *X:202–4*

❧ WILL WONDER become extinct in me? Shall I become insensible as a fungus?

A ridge of earth, with the red cockscomb lichen on it, peeps out still at the rut's edge. The dear wholesome color of shrub oak leaves, so clean and firm, not decaying, but which have put on a kind of immortality, not wrinkled and thin like the white oak leaves, but full-veined and plump, as nearer earth. Well-tanned leather on the one side, sun-tanned, color of colors, color of the cow and the deer, silver-downy beneath, turned toward the late bleached and russet fields. What are acanthus leaves and the rest to this? Emblem of my winter condition. I love and could embrace the shrub oak with its scanty garment of leaves rising above the snow, lowly whispering to me, akin to winter thoughts, and sunsets, and to all virtue. Covert which the hare and the partridge seek, and I too seek. What cousin of mine is the shrub oak? How can any man suffer long? For a sense of want is a prayer, and all prayers are answered. Rigid as iron, clean as the atmosphere, hardy as virtue, innocent and sweet as a maiden is the shrub oak. In proportion as I know and love it, I am natural and sound as a partridge. I felt a positive yearning toward one bush this afternoon. There was a match found for me at last. I fell in love with a shrub oak.

1 December 1856, Journal *IX:145–46*

❦ MY THEMES shall not be far-fetched. I will tell of homely every-day phenomena and adventures. Friends! Society! It seems to me that I have an abundance[;] . . . there is so much that I rejoice and sympathize with, and men, too, that I never speak to but only know and think of. What you call bareness and poverty is to me simplicity. God could not be unkind to me if he should try. I love the winter, with its imprisonment and its cold, for it compels the prisoner to try new fields and resources. I love to have the river closed up for a season and a pause put to my boating, to be obliged to get my boat in. I shall launch it again in the spring with so much more pleasure. This is an advantage in point of abstinence and moderation compared with the seaside boating, where the boat ever lies on the shore. I love best to have each thing in its season only, and enjoy doing without it at all other times. It is the greatest of all advantages to enjoy no advantage at all. I find it invariably true, the poorer I am, the richer I am. What you consider my disadvantage, I consider my advantage. While you are pleased to get knowledge and culture in many ways, I am delighted to think that I am getting rid of them. I have never got over my surprise that I should have been born into the most estimable place in all the world, and in the very nick of time, too.

5 December 1856, Journal *IX:160*

❦ TO WALDEN.

Snowed yesterday afternoon, and now it is three or four inches deep and a fine mizzle falling and freezing to the twigs and stubble, so that there is quite a glaze. The stiffened ice-coated weeds and grasses on the causeway recall past winters.

These humble withered plants, which have not of late attracted your attention, now arrest it by their very stiffness and exaggerated size. Some grass culms eighteen inches or two feet high, which nobody noticed, are an inexhaustible supply of slender ice-wands set in the snow. The grasses and weeds bent to the crusty surface form arches of various forms. It is surprising how the slenderest grasses can support such a weight, but the culm is buttressed by another icy culm or column, and the load gradually taken on. In the woods the drooping pines compel you to stoop. In all directions they are bowed down, hanging their heads. The birches are still upright, and their numerous parallel white ice-rods remind me of the recent gossamer-like gleams which they reflected.

5 December 1858, Journal *XI:364–65*

❦ To READ to a promiscuous audience who are at your mercy the fine thoughts you solaced yourself with far away is as violent as to fatten geese by cramming, and in this case they do not get fatter. . . .

Winter has come unnoticed by me, I have been so busy writing [lectures]. This is the life most lead in respect to Nature. How different from my habitual one! It is hasty, coarse, and trivial, as if you were a spindle in a factory. The other is leisurely, fine, and glorious, like a flower. In the first case you are merely getting your living; in the second you live as you go along. You travel only on roads of the proper grade without jar or running off the track, and sweep round the hills by beautiful curves.

6, 8 December 1854, Journal *VII:80*

❦ THAT GRAND OLD POEM called Winter is round again without any connivance of mine. . . . It seemed as if winter had come without any interval since midsummer, and I was prepared to see it flit away by the time I again looked over my shoulder. It was as if I had dreamed it. But I see the farmers have had time to gather their harvests as usual, and the seasons have revolved as slowly as in the first autumn of my life. The winters come now as fast as snowflakes. It is wonderful that old men do not lose their reckoning. It was summer, and now again it is winter. Nature loves this rhyme so well that she never tires of repeating it. So sweet and wholesome is the winter, so simple and moderate, so satisfactory and perfect, that her children will never weary of it. What a poem! an epic in blank verse, enriched with a million tinkling rhymes. It is solid beauty. It has been subjected to the vicissitudes of millions of years of the gods, and not a single superfluous ornament remains.

7 December 1856, Journal *IX:167–68*

❦ SUDDENLY COLD LAST NIGHT. The river and Fair Haven Pond froze over *generally* . . . last night, though they were only frozen along the edges yesterday. This is unusually sudden. . . .

I observe at mid-afternoon, the air being very quiet and serene, that peculiarly softened western sky, which is perhaps seen commonly after the first snow has covered the earth. There are many whitish filmy clouds a third of the way to the zenith, generally long and narrow, parallel with the horizon, with indistinct edges, alternating with the blue. And there is just enough *invisible* vapor, perhaps from the snow, to soften the blue, giving it a slight greenish tinge. Thus, methinks, it often happens that as the weather is harder the sky seems softer. It is not a cold, hard, glittering sky, but a warm, soft, filmy one.

The prosaic man sees things baldly, or with the bodily sense; but the poet sees them clad in beauty, with the spiritual sense.

9 December 1859, Journal *XIII:18*

❦ To PERCEIVE FRESHLY, with fresh senses, is to be inspired. . . .

My body is all sentient. As I go here or there, I am tickled by this or that I come in contact with, as if I touched the wires of a battery. I can generally recall—have fresh in my mind—several scratches last received. These I continually recall to mind, reimpress, and harp upon. The age of miracles is each moment thus returned. Now it is wild apples, now river reflections, now a flock of lesser redpolls. In winter, too, resides immortal youth and perennial summer. Its head is not silvered; its cheek is not blanched but has a ruby tinge to it.

If any part of nature excites our pity, it is for ourselves we grieve, for there is eternal health and beauty. We get only transient and partial glimpses of the beauty of the world. Standing at the right angle, we are dazzled by the colors of the rainbow in colorless ice. From the right point of view, every storm and every drop in it is a rainbow. Beauty and music are not mere traits and exceptions. They are the rule and character. It is the exception that we see and hear. Then I try to discover what it was in the vision that charmed and translated me. What if we could daguerreotype our thoughts and feelings! for I am surprised and enchanted often by some quality which I cannot detect. I have seen an attribute of another world and condition of things. It is a wonderful fact that I should be affected, and thus deeply and powerfully, more than by aught else in all my experience,—that this fruit should be borne in me, sprung from a seed finer than the spores of fungi, floated from other atmospheres! finer than the dust caught in the sails of vessels a thousand miles from land! Here the invisible seeds settle, and spring, and bear flowers and fruits of immortal beauty.

11 December 1855, Journal *VIII:44–45*

❦ A MILD SUMMER SUN shines over forest and lake— The earth looks as fair this morning as the valhalla of the gods— Indeed our spirits never go beyond nature. In the woods there is an inexpressible happiness— Their mirth is [just] repressed.

In winter, when there is but one green leaf for many rods, what warm content is in them— They are not rude but tender even in the severest cold. Their nakedness is their defence. All their sounds and sights are elixir to my spirit. They possess a divine health God is not more well. Every sound is inspiriting—and frawght with the same mysterious assurance from the creaking of the boughs in January to the soft sugh of the wind in July. . . .

I seem to see somewhat more of my own kith and kin in the lichens on the rocks than in any books It does seem as if mine were a peculiarly wild nature—which so yearns toward all wildness—. I know of no redeeming qualities in me—but a sincere love for some things— And when I am reproved I have to fall back on to this ground.

This is my argument in reserve for all cases. My love is invulnerable[;] meet me on that ground, and you will find me

strong. When I am condemned and condemn myself utterly—I
think straightway—but I rely on my love for some things.
Therein I am whole and entire. Therein I am God-propt.

15 December 1841, Journal *1:343–45*

😃 F ROZEN M IST. The woods were this morning covered with
thin bars of vapor—the evaporation of the leaves . . . which
seemed to have been suddenly stiffened by the cold. In some
places it was spread out like gauze over the tops of the trees,
forming extended lawns, where elves and fairies held high tour-
nament

16 December 1837, Journal *1:18–19*

WINTER

 I WANT TO GO SOON and live away by the pond where I shall hear only the wind whispering among the reeds— It will be success if I shall have left myself behind But my friends ask what I will do when I get there? Will it not be employment enough to watch the progress of the seasons?

24 December 1841, Journal *1:347*

 WE MUST GO OUT and re-ally ourselves to Nature every day. We must make root, send out some little fibre at least, even every winter day. I am sensible that I am imbibing health when I open my mouth to the wind. Staying in the house breeds a sort of insanity always. Every house is in this sense a hospital. A night and a forenoon is as much confinement to those wards as I can stand. I am aware that I recover some sanity which I had almost lost the instant that I come abroad.

29 December 1856, Journal *IX:200*

 IT IS A REMARKABLE SIGHT, this snow-clad landscape, with the fences and bushes half buried and the warm sun on it. The snow lies not quite level in the fields, but in low waves with an abrupt edge on the north or wind side, as it lodges on ice.

The town and country are now so still, there being no rattle
of wagons nor even jingle of sleigh-bells, every tread being as
with woolen feet. . . . There are a few sounds . . . which never
fail to affect me. The notes of the wood thrush and the sound
of a vibrating chord, these affect me as many sounds once did
often, and as almost all should. The strains of the æolian harp
and of the wood thrush are the truest and loftiest preachers that
I know now left on this earth. I know of no missionaries to us
heathen comparable to them. They, as it were, lift us up in spite
of ourselves. They intoxicate, they charm us. Where was that
strain mixed into which this world was dropped but as a lump of
sugar to sweeten the draught? I would be drunk, drunk, drunk,
dead drunk to this world with it forever. He that hath ears, let
him hear[;] . . . the hearing of it makes men brave.

31 December 1853, Journal *VI:38–39*

❧ THE SNOW IS THE GREAT BETRAYER. It not only shows the
tracks of mice, otters, etc., etc., which else we should rarely if
ever see, but the tree sparrows are more plainly seen against its
white ground, and they in turn are attracted by the dark weeds
which it reveals. It also drives the crows and other birds out of
the woods to the villages for food. We might expect to find in
the snow the footprint of a life superior to our own, of which
no zoölogy takes cognizance. Is there no trace of a nobler life
than that of an otter or an escaped convict to be looked for in
the snow? Shall we suppose that that is the only life that has
been abroad in the night? It is only the savage that can see the
track of no higher life than an otter. Why do the vast snow
plains give us pleasure, the twilight of the bent and half-buried

woods? Is not all there consonant with virtue, justice, purity, courage, magnanimity? Are we not cheered by the sight? And does not all this amount to the track of a higher life than the otter's, a life which has not gone by and left a footprint merely, but is there with its beauty, its music, its perfume, its sweetness, to exhilarate and recreate us? Where there is a perfect government of the world according to the highest laws, is there no trace of intelligence there, whether in the snow or the earth, or in ourselves? No other trail but such as a dog can smell? Is there none which an angel can detect and follow? None to guide a man on his pilgrimage, which water will not conceal? Is there no odor of sanctity to be perceived? Is its trail too old? Have mortals lost the scent? . . . Did this great snow come to reveal the track merely of some timorous hare, or of the Great Hare, whose track no hunter has seen? Is there no trace nor suggestion of Purity to be detected? If one could detect the meaning of the snow, would he not be on the trail of some higher life that has been abroad in the night? Are there not hunters who seek for something higher than foxes, with judgment more discriminating than the senses of fox-hounds, who rally to a nobler music than that of the hunting-horn? As there is contention among the fishermen who shall be the first to reach the pond as soon as the ice will bear, . . . as the hunters are forward to take the field as soon as the first snow has fallen, so the observer, or he who would make the most of his life . . . must be abroad early and late, in spite of cold and wet, in pursuit of nobler game, whose traces are then most distinct. A life which, pursued, does not earth itself, does not burrow downward but upward, which takes not to the trees but to the heavens as its home, which the hunter pursues with winged thoughts and aspirations,—these the dogs that tree it,—rallying his pack with the bugle notes of undying faith, and returns with some worthier trophy than a fox's tail, a life which we seek, not to destroy it, but to save our own. Is the great snow of use to the hunter only, and not to the saint, or him who is earnestly building up a life?

1 January 1854, Journal *VI:43–45*

❧ NATURE WORKS with such luxuriance & fury that she follows the least hint. And on the twigs of bushes for each bud there is a corresponding icy swelling. The bells are particularly sweet this morning. I hear more methinks than ever before. How much more religion in their sound, than they ever call men together to—men obey their call & go to the stove-warmed church—though God exhibits himself to the walker in a frosted bush today as much as in a burning one to Moses of old. . . .

The world is a crystal palace. The trees stiff & drooping and encased in ice looked as if they were sculptured in marble. . . . I love nature partly *because* she is not man, but a retreat from him. None of his institutions control or pervade her. There a different kind of right prevails. In her midst I can be glad with an entire gladness. If this world was all man I could not stretch myself— I should lose all hope. He is constraint; she is freedom to me. He makes me wish for another world— She makes me content with this.

2-3 January 1853, Journal *5:420–22*

Winter

❧ THE THIN SNOW now driving from the north and lodging on my coat consists of those beautiful star crystals, not cottony and chubby spokes, . . . but thin and partly transparent crystals. They are about a tenth of an inch in diameter, perfect little wheels with six spokes without a tire, or rather with six perfect little leafets, fern-like, with a distinct straight and slender midrib, raying from the centre. . . . How full of the creative genius is the air in which these are generated! I should hardly admire more if real stars fell and lodged on my coat. Nature is full of genius, full of the divinity; so that not a snowflake escapes its fashioning hand. Nothing is cheap and coarse, neither dewdrops nor snowflakes. Soon the storm increases, . . . and the snow comes finer, more white and powdery. Who knows but this is the original form of all snowflakes, but that when I observe these crystal stars falling around me they are but just generated in the low mist next the earth? I am nearer to the source of the snow, its primal, auroral, and golden hour or infancy, but commonly the flakes reach us travel-worn and agglomerated, comparatively without order or beauty, far down in their fall, like men in their advanced age. . . .

A divinity must have stirred within them before the crystals did thus shoot and set. Wheels of the storm-chariots. The same law that shapes the earth-star shapes the snow-star. As surely as the petals of a flower are fixed, each of these countless snow-stars comes whirling to earth, pronouncing thus, with emphasis, the number six. . . .

. . . What a world we live in! where myriads of these little disks, so beautiful to the most prying eye, are whirled down on every traveller's coat, the observant and the unobservant, and on the restless squirrel's fur, and on the far-stretching fields and forests, the wooded dells, and the mountain-tops. Far, far away from the haunts of man, they roll down some little slope, fall over and come to their bearings, and melt or lose their beauty in the mass, ready anon to swell some little rill with their contribution, and so, at last, the universal ocean from which they came. There they lie, like the wreck of chariot-wheels after a battle in the skies. Meanwhile the meadow mouse shoves them aside in his gallery, the school boy casts them in his snowball, or the woodman's sled glides smoothly over them, these glorious spangles, the sweeping of heaven's floor. And they all sing, melting as they sing of the mysteries of the number six,—six, six, six. He takes up the water of the sea in his hand, leaving the salt; He disperses it in mist through the skies; He recollects and sprinkles it like grain in six-rayed snowy stars over the earth, there to lie till He dissolves its bonds again.

5 January 1856, Journal *VIII:87–89*

❦ A MAN RECEIVES only what he is ready to receive, whether physically or intellectually or morally, as animals conceive at certain seasons their kind only. We hear and apprehend only what we already half know. If there is something which does not concern me, which is out of my line, which by experience or by genius my attention is not drawn to, however novel and remarkable it may be, if it is spoken, we hear it not, if it is written, we read it not, or if we read it, it does not detain us. Every man thus *tracks himself* through life, in all his hearing and reading and observation and travelling. His observations make a chain. The phenomenon or fact that cannot in any wise be linked with the rest which he has observed, he does not observe. By and by we may be ready to receive what we cannot receive now.

5 January 1860, Journal *XIII:77*

Nature [has] not lost her pristine vigor yet, ... why should man lose heart? ... What a world we live in! Where are the jewellers' shops? There is nothing handsomer than a snowflake and a dewdrop. I may say that the maker of the world exhausts his skill with each snowflake and dewdrop that he sends down.

6 January 1858, Journal *X:239*

❦ I AM SINGULARLY REFRESHED in winter when I hear tell of service berries—poke-weed—Juniper— Is not heaven made up of these cheap summer glories?

The great God is very calm withall. How superfluous is any excitement in his creatures! He listens equally to the prayers of the believer and the unbeliever—

The moods of man should unfold and alternate as gradually and as placidly as those of nature The sun shines for aye! The sudden revolutions of these times and this generation, have acquired a very exaggerated importance— They do not interest me much—for they are not in harmony with the longer periods of nature. The present, in any aspect in which it can be presented to the smallest audience, is always mean. God does not sympathize with the popular movements.

7 January 1842, Journal *1:360*

❦ I GO THROUGH THE WOODS toward the Cliffs along the side of the Well Meadow Field.

There is nothing so sanative, so poetic, as a walk in the woods and fields even now, when I meet none abroad for pleasure. Nothing so inspires me and excites such serene and profitable thought. The objects are elevating. In the street and in society I am almost invariably cheap and dissipated, my life unspeakably mean. No amount of gold or respectability would in the least redeem it . . . But alone in distant woods or fields, in unpretending sprout-lands or pastures tracked by rabbits, even in a bleak and, to most, cheerless day, like this, when a villager would be thinking of his inn, I come to myself, I once more feel myself grandly related, and that cold and solitude are friends of mine. I suppose that this value, in my case, is equivalent to what others get by churchgoing and prayer. I come to my solitary woodland walk as the homesick go home. I thus dispose of the superfluous and see things as they are, grand and beautiful. I have told many that I walk every day about half the daylight. . . . I wish to get the Concord, the Massachusetts, the America, out of my head and be sane a part of every day. If there are missionaries for the heathen, why not send them to me? I wish to know something; I wish to be made better. I wish to forget, a considerable part of every day, all mean, narrow, trivial men . . . and therefore I come out to these solitudes, where the problem of existence is simplified. I get away a mile or two from the town into the stillness and solitude of nature, with rocks, trees, weeds, snow about me. I enter some glade in the woods, perchance, where a few weeds and dry leaves alone lift themselves above the surface of the snow, and it is as if I had come to an open window. I see out and around myself. Our *skylights* are thus far away from the ordinary resorts of men. I am not satisfied with ordinary windows. I must have a true *skylight*. My true skylight is on the outside of the village. I am not thus expanded, recreated, enlightened, when I meet a company of men. . . . They bore me. The man I meet with is not often so instructive as the silence he breaks. This stillness, solitude, wildness of nature is a kind of thoroughwort, or boneset, to my intellect. This is what I go out to seek. It is as if I always met in those places some grand, serene, immortal, infinitely encouraging, though invisible, companion, and walked with him. There at last my nerves are steadied, my senses and my mind do their office. I am aware that most of my neighbors would think it a hardship to be compelled to linger here one hour, especially this bleak day, and yet I receive this sweet and ineffable compensation for it. It is the most agreeable thing I do. . . .

I love and celebrate nature, even in detail, merely because I love the scenery of these interviews and translations. I love to remember every creature that was at this *club*. I thus get off a certain social scurf and scaliness. I do not consider the other animals brutes in the common sense. I am attracted toward them undoubtedly because I never heard any nonsense from them. I have not convicted them of folly, or vanity, or pomposity, or stupidity, in dealing with me. . . . My fairies invariably take to flight when a man appears upon the scene. In a caucus, a meeting-house, a lyceum, a club-room, there is nothing like it in my experience. But away out of the town, on Brown's scrub oak lot, which was sold the other day for six dollars an acre, I have company such as England cannot buy, nor afford. This society is what I live, what I survey, for. I subscribe generously to *this*—all that I have and am.

There, in that Well Meadow Field, perhaps, I feel in my element again, as when a fish is put back into the water. I wash off all my chagrins. All things go smoothly as the axle of the universe. I can remember that when I was very young I used to have a dream night after night, over and over again, which might have been named Rough and Smooth. All existence, all satisfaction and dissatisfaction, all event was symbolized in this way. Now I seemed to be lying and tossing, perchance, on a horrible, a fatal rough surface, which must soon, indeed, put an end to my existence, though even in the dream I knew it to be the symbol merely of my misery; and then again, suddenly, I was lying on a delicious smooth surface, as of a summer sea, as of gossamer or down or softest plush, and life was such a luxury to live. My waking experience *always* has been and is such an alternate Rough and Smooth. In other words it is Insanity and Sanity.

Might I aspire to praise the moderate nymph Nature! I must be like her, moderate.

7 *January 1857*, Journal *IX:208–11*

❦ AFTER A SPITTING of snow in the forenoon, I see the blue sky here and there, and the sun is coming out. It is still and warm. The earth is two thirds bare. I walk along the Mill Brook below Emerson's, looking into it for some life.

Perhaps what most moves us in winter is some reminiscence of far-off summer. How we leap by the side of the open brooks! What beauty in the running brooks! What life! What society! The cold is merely superficial; it is summer still at the core, far, far within. It is in the cawing of the crow, the crowing of the cock, the warmth of the sun on our backs. I hear faintly the cawing of a crow far, far away, echoing from some unseen wood-side, as if deadened by the springlike vapor which the sun is drawing from the ground. It mingles with the slight murmur of the village, the sound of children at play, as one stream empties gently into another, and the wild and tame are one. What a delicious sound! It is not merely crow calling to crow, for it

speaks to me too. I am part of one great creature with him; if
he has voice, I have ears. I can hear when he calls, and have
engaged not to shoot nor stone him if he will caw to me each
spring. On the one hand, it may be, is the sound of children
at school saying their a, b, ab's, on the other, far in the wood-
fringed horizon, the cawing of crows from their blessed eternal
vacation, out at their long recess, children who have got dis-
missed! While the vaporous incense goes up from all the fields
of spring—if it were spring. Ah, bless the Lord, O my soul!
bless him for wildness, for crows that will not alight within
gunshot! and bless him for hens, too, that croak and cackle in
the yard!

12 January 1855, Journal *VII:112–13*

❧ IT IS THE DISCOVERY of science that stupendous changes in
the earth's surface, such as are referred to the Deluge, for instance, are the result of causes still in operation, which have
been at work for an incalculable period. There has not been a
sudden re-formation, or, as it were, new creation of the world,
but a steady progress according to existing laws. The same is
true in detail also. It is a vulgar prejudice that some plants are
"spontaneously generated," but science knows that they come
from seeds, *i.e.* are the result of causes still in operation, however slow and unobserved. It is a common saying that "little
strokes fall great oaks," and it does not imply much wisdom in
him who originated it. The sound of the axe invites our attention to such a catastrophe; we can easily count each stroke as it
is given, and all the neighborhood is informed by a loud crash
when the deed is consummated. But such, too, is the rise of the

oak; little strokes of a different kind and often repeated raise great oaks, but scarcely a traveller hears these or turns aside to converse with Nature, who is dealing them the while.

Nature is slow but sure; she works no faster than need be; she is the tortoise that wins the race by her perseverance; she knows that seeds have many other uses than to reproduce their kind. In raising oaks and pines, she works with a leisureliness and security answering to the age and strength of the trees. If every acorn of this year's crop is destroyed, never fear! she has more years to come. It is not necessary that a pine or an oak should bear fruit every year, as it is that a pea-vine should. So . . . the greatest changes in the landscape are produced more gradually than we expected. If Nature has a pine or an oak wood to produce, she manifests no haste about it.

14 January 1861, Journal *XIV:311–12*

❧ IN PROPORTION as I have celestial thoughts, is the necessity for me to be out and behold the western sky before sunset these winter days. That is the symbol of the unclouded mind that knows neither winter nor summer. What is your thought like? That is the hue—that the purity & transparency and distance from earthly taint of my inmost mind—for whatever we see without is a symbol of something within—& that which is farthest off—is the symbol of what is deepest within. The lover of contemplation accordingly will gaze much into the sky.— Fair thoughts & a serene mind make fair days.

17 January 1852, Journal *4:263*

❦ EVERY ONE, no doubt, has looked with delight, holding his face low, at that beautiful frostwork which so frequently in winter mornings is seen bristling about the throat of every breathing-hole in the earth's surface. In this case the fog, the earth's breath made visible, was in such abundance that it invested all our vales and hills, and the frostwork, accordingly, instead of being confined to the chinks and crannies of the earth, covered the mightiest trees, so that we, walking beneath them, had the same wonderful prospect and environment that an insect would have in the former case. We, going along our roads, had such a prospect as an insect would have making its way through a chink in the earth which was bristling with hoar frost.

That glaze! I know what it was by my own experience; it was the frozen breath of the earth upon its beard. . . . Closely examined, it is a coarse aggregation of thin flakes or leaflets. . . .

Take the most rigid tree, the whole effect is peculiarly soft and spirit-like, for there is no marked edge or outline. How could you draw the outline of these snowy fingers against the fog, without exaggeration? There is no more a boundary-line or circumference that can be drawn, than a diameter. Hardly could the New England farmer drive to market under these trees without feeling that his sense of beauty was addressed. He would be aware that the phenomenon called beauty was become visible, if one were at leisure or had had the right culture to appreciate it. . . . [A] farmer told me in all sincerity that, having occasion to go into Walden Woods in his sleigh, he thought he never saw anything so beautiful in all his life, and if there had been men there who knew how to write about it, it would have been a great occasion for them.

Many times I thought that if the particular tree . . . under which I was walking or riding were the only one like it in the country, it would [be] worth a journey across the continent to see it. Indeed, I have no doubt that such journeys would be undertaken on hearing a true account of it. But, instead of being confined to a single tree, this wonder was as cheap and common as the air itself. Every man's woodlot was a miracle and surprise to him, and for those who could not go so far there were the trees in and street and the weeds in the yard. It was much like (in effect) that snow that lodges on the fine dead twigs on the lower part of a pine wood, resting there in the twilight commonly only till it has done snowing and the wind arises. But in this case it did not rest *on* the twig, but . . . covered the whole forest and every surface.

18 January 1859, Journal *XI:404–6*

❦ THERE WAS A HIGH WIND last night, which relieved the trees of their burden almost entirely, but I may still see the drifts. The surface of the snow everywhere in the fields, where it is hard blown, has a fine grain with low shelves, like slate stone that does not split well. We cross the fields behind Hubbard's and suddenly slump into dry ditches concealed by the snow, up to the middle, and flounder out again. How new all things seem! Here is a broad, shallow pool in the fields, which yesterday was slosh, now converted into a soft, white, fleecy snow ice, like bread that has spewed out and baked outside the pan. It is like the beginning of the world. There is nothing hackneyed where a new snow can come and cover all the landscape. . . .

The world is not only new to the eye, but is still as at creation; every blade and leaf is hushed; not a bird or insect is heard; only, perchance, a faint tinkling sleigh-bell in the distance.

20 January 1855, Journal *7:123–24*

❧ EVERY LEAF AND TWIG was this morning covered with a sparkling ice armor, even the grasses in exposed fields were hung with innumerable diamond pendents, which jingled merrily when brushed by the foot of the traveller. It was literally the wreck of jewels and the crash of gems— It was as though some superincumbent stratum of the earth had been removed in the night—exposing to light a bed of untarnished crystals. The scene changed at every step—or as the head was inclined to the right or the left— There were the opal—and sapphire— and emerald—and jasper—and beryl—and topaz—and ruby.

Such is the beauty ever—neither here nor there, now nor then—neither in Rome nor in Athens—but wherever there is a soul to admire. If I seek her elsewhere because I do not find her at home, my search will prove a fruitless one.

21 January 1838, Journal *1:26*

❧ TO INSURE HEALTH, a man's relation to Nature must come very near to a personal one; he must be conscious of a friendliness in her; when human friends fail or die, she must stand in the gap to him. I cannot conceive of any life which deserves the name, unless there is a certain tender relation to Nature. This it is which makes winter warm, and supplies society in the desert and wilderness. Unless Nature sympathizes with and speaks to us, as it were, the most fertile and blooming regions are barren and dreary.

23 January 1858, Journal *X:252*

❦ A SHARP CUTTING AIR— This is a pretty good winter morning however— ... There are from time to time mornings—both
in summer & winter when especially the world seems to begin
anew—beyond which memory need not go—for not behind
them is yesterday and our past life—when as in the morning
of a hoar frost there are visible the effects of a certain creative
energy—the world has visibly been recreated in the night—
mornings of creation I call them.

In the midst of these marks of a creative energy recently
active—while the sun is rising with more than usual splendor I look back—I look back for the era of this creation not
into the night but to a dawn for which no man ever rose early
enough. A morning which carries us back beyond the Mosaic
creation—where crystallizations are fresh & unmelted. It is the
poet's hour. Mornings when men are new born—men who have
the seeds of life in them. It should be a part of my religion to
[be] abroad then.

26 January 1853, Journal *5:453–54*

❦ IT IS SO MILD and moist as I saunter along by the wall east of
the Hill that I remember, or anticipate, one of those warm rain-
storms in the spring, when the earth is just laid bare, the wind
is south, and the cladonia lichens are swollen and lusty with
moisture, your foot sinking into them and pressing the water
out as from a sponge, and the sandy places also are drinking
it in. You wander indefinitely in a beaded coat, wet to the skin
of your legs, sit on moss-clad rocks and stumps, and hear the
lisping of migrating sparrows flitting amid the shrub oaks, sit
long at a time, still, and have your thoughts. A rain which is

as serene as fair weather, suggesting fairer weather than was ever seen. You could hug the clods that defile you. You feel the fertilizing influence of the rain in your mind. The part of you that is wettest is fullest of life, like the lichens. You discover evidences of immortality not known to divines. You cease to die. You detect some buds and sprouts of life. Every step in the old rye-field is on virgin soil.

And then the rain comes thicker and faster than before, thawing the remaining frost in the ground, detaining the migrating bird; and you turn your back to it, full of serene, contented thought, soothed by the steady dropping on the withered leaves, more at home for being abroad, more comfortable for being wet, sinking at each step deep into the thawing earth, gladly breaking through the gray rotting ice. . . . You cannot go home yet; you stay and sit in the rain. You glide along the distant wood-side, full of joy and expectation, seeing nothing but beauty, hearing nothing but music, as free as the fox-colored sparrow, seeing far ahead, a courageous knight, a great philosopher, not indebted to any academy or college for this expansion, but chiefly to the April rain, which descendeth on all alike.

27 January 1858, Journal X:262–63

❧ WHAT FINE AND PURE REDS we see in the sunset sky! Yet earth is not ransacked for dye-stuffs. It is all accomplished by the sunlight on vapor at the right angle, and the sunset is constant if you are at the right angle. The sunset sky is sometimes more northerly, sometimes more southerly. I saw one the other day occupying only the southern horizon, but very fine, and reaching more than half-way to the zenith from west to east. . . .

As I go along the edge of Hubbard's Wood, on the ice, it is very warm in the sun—and calm there. There are certain spots I could name, by hill and wood sides, which are always thus sunny and warm in fair weather, and have been, for aught I know, since the world was made. What a distinction they enjoy!

How many memorable localities in a river walk! Here is the warm wood-side; next, the good fishing bay; and next, where the old settler was drowned when crossing on the ice a hundred years ago. It is all storied. . . .

These winter days I occasionally hear the note of a goldfinch, or maybe a redpoll, unseen, passing high overhead.

When you think that your walk is profitless and a failure, and you can hardly persuade yourself not to return, it is on the point of being a success, for then you are in that subdued and knocking mood to which Nature never fails to open.

27 January 1860, Journal *XIII:110–11*

❦ THE SNOW COLLECTS upon the plumes of the pitch pine in the form of a pineapple, which if you divide in the middle will expose three red kernels like the tamarind stone. . . .

The snow falls on no two trees alike, but the forms it assumes are as various as those of the twigs and leaves which receive it. They are as it were predetermined by the genius of the tree. So one divine spirit descends alike on all, but bears a peculiar fruit in each. The divinity subsides on all men, as the snow flakes settle on the fields, and ledges, and take the form of the various clefts and surfaces in which it lodges.

30 January 1841, Journal *1:238–40*

Winter

❦ THE WINTER, cold and bound out as it is, is thrown to us like a bone to a famishing dog, and we are expected to get the marrow out of it. While the milkmen in the outskirts are milking so many scores of cows before sunrise these winter mornings, it is our task to milk the winter itself. It is true it is like a cow that is dry, and our fingers are numb, and there is none to wake us up. Some desert the field and go into winter quarters in the city. They attend the oratorios, while the only music that we countrymen hear is the squeaking of the snow under our boots. But the winter was not given to us for no purpose. We must thaw its cold with our genialness. We are tasked to find out and appropriate all the nutriment it yields. If it is a cold and hard season, its fruit, no doubt, is the more concentrated and nutty. It took the cold and bleakness of November to ripen the walnut, but the human brain is the kernel which the winter itself matures. Not till then does its shell come off. The seasons were not made in vain. Because the fruits of the earth are already ripe, we are not to suppose that there is no fruit left for winter to ripen. It is for man the seasons and all their fruits exist. The winter was made to concentrate and harden and mature the kernel of his brain, to give tone and firmness and consistency to his thought. Then is the great harvest of the year, the harvest of thought. All previous harvests are stubble to this, mere fodder and green crop. Now we burn with a purer flame like the stars; our oil is winter-strained. We are islanded in Atlantic and Pacific and Indian Oceans of thought, Bermudas, or Friendly or Spice Islands.

30 January 1854, Journal *VI:84–85*

❧ To MAKE A PERFECT winter day like this, you must have a clear, sparkling air, with a sheen from the snow, sufficient cold, little or no wind; and the warmth must come directly from the sun. It must not be a thawing warmth. The tension of nature must not be relaxed. The earth must be resonant if bare, and you hear the lisping tinkle of chickadees from time to time and the unrelenting steel-cold scream of a jay, unmelted, that never flows into a song, a sort of wintry trumpet, screaming cold; hard, tense, frozen music, like the winter sky itself; in the blue livery of winter's band. It is like a flourish of trumpets to the winter sky. There is no hint of incubation in the jay's scream. Like the creak of a cart-wheel. There is no cushion for sounds now. They tear our ears.

12 February 1854, Journal *VI:118*

❧ CONSIDER THE FARMER, who is commonly regarded as the healthiest man— He may be the toughest but he is not the healthiest. He has lost his elasticity—he can neither run nor jump— Health is the free use & command of all our faculties— & equal development— His is the health of the ox—an over worked buffalo— His joints are stiff. The resemblance is true even in particulars. He is cast away in a pair of cowhide boots— and travels at an ox's pace—indeed in some places he puts his foot into the skin of an ox's shin. It would do him good to be thoroughly shampooed to make him supple. His health is an insensibility to all influence— But only the healthiest man in the world is sensible to the finest influence— He who is affected by more or less of electricity in the air—

We shall see but little way if we require to understand what we see— How few things can a man measure with the tape of his understanding—how many greater things might he . . . be seeing in the meanwhile.

One afternoon in the fall . . . I saw Fair Haven Pond with its island & meadow[;] between the island and the shore, a strip of perfectly smooth water in the lee of the island & two hawks sailing over it—(and something more I saw which cannot easily be described which made me say to myself that the landscape could not be improved.) I did not see how it could be improved. Yet I do not know what these things can be; (for) I begin to see such objects only when I leave off understanding them—and afterwards remember that I did not appreciate them before. But I get no further than this. How adapted these forms & colors to our eyes, a meadow & its islands. What are these things? Yet the hawks & the ducks keep so aloof, & nature is so reserved! We are made to love the river & the meadow as the wind (is made) to ripple the water

14 February 1851, Journal *3:192–93*

❦ ALL DAY a steady, warm, imprisoning rain carrying off the snow, not unmusical on my roof. It is a rare time for the student and reader who cannot go abroad in the afternoon, provided he can keep awake, for we are wont to be drowsy as cats in such weather. Without, it is not walking but wading. It is so long since I have heard it that the steady, soaking, rushing sound of the rain on the shingles is musical. The fire needs no replenishing, and we save our fuel. It seems like a distant forerunner of spring. It is because I am allied to the elements that the sound of the rain is thus soothing to me. The sound soaks into my spirit, as the water into the earth, reminding me of the season when snow and ice will be no more, when the earth will be thawed and drink up the rain as fast as it falls.

15 February 1855, Journal *VII:186*

❧ I HAVE A COMMON PLACE BOOK for facts and another for poetry—but I find it difficult always to preserve the vague distinction which I had in my mind—for the most interesting & beautiful facts are so much the more poetry and that is their success. They are *translated* from earth to heaven— I see that if my facts were sufficiently vital & significant—perhaps transmuted more into the substance of the human mind—I should need but one book of poetry to contain them all.

18 February 1852, Journal *4:356*

❧ THE STRAINS FROM MY MUSE are as rare now a days—or of late years—as the notes of birds in the winter—the faintest occasional tinkling sound.— & mostly of the woodpecker kind—or the harsh jay or crow. It never melts into a song. Only the day-day-day of an inquisitive titmouse.

Everywhere snow—gathered into sloping drifts about the walls & fences—& beneath the snow the frozen ground—and men are compelled to deposit the summer's provision in burrows in the earth like the ground-squirrel. Many creatures daunted by the prospect migrated in the fall, but man remains

and walks over the frozen snow crust—and over the stiffened
rivers & ponds. & draws now upon his summer stores. Life is
reduced to its lowest terms. There is no home for you now—
in this freezing wind but in that shelter which you prepared
in the summer— You steer straight across the fields to that
in season. I can with difficulty tell when I am over the river.
There is a similar crust over my heart. Where I rambled in the
summer—& gathered flowers and rested on the grass by the
brookside in the shade—now no grass nor flowers—nor brook
nor shade—but cold unvaried snow stretching mile after mile
and no place to sit.

19 February 1852, Journal *4:357–58*

❦ WHAT IS THE RELATION between a bird and the ear that
appreciates its melody, to whom, perchance, it is more charming
and significant than to any else? Certainly they are intimately
related, and the one was made for the other. It is a natural fact.
If I were to discover that a certain kind of stone by the pond-
shore was affected, say partially disintegrated, by a particular
natural sound, as of a bird or insect, I see that one could not be
completely described without describing the other. I am that
rock by the pond-side.

What is hope, what is expectation, but a seed-time whose
harvest cannot fail, an irresistible expedition of the mind, at
length to be victorious?

20 February 1857, Journal *IX:274–75*

❦ MEASURE YOUR HEALTH by your sympathy with morning and spring. If there is no response in you to the awakening of nature,—if the prospect of an early morning walk does not banish sleep, if the warble of the first bluebird does not thrill you,—know that the morning and spring of your life are past. Thus may you feel your pulse.

25 February 1859, Journal *XI:455*

❦ I HEAR A MAN BLOWING A HORN this still evening—and it sounds like the plaint of nature in these times. In this which I refer to some man there is something greater than any man It is as if the earth spoke. It adds a great remoteness to the horizon, and its very distance is grand, as when one draws back the head to speak. That which I now hear in the west seems like an invitation to the east. . . . It is the spirit of the West calling to the spirit of the East or else it is the rattling of some team lagging in Days' train coming to me through the darkness and silence. . . .

It is a strangely healthy sound for these disjointed times.— It is a rare soundness when cow-bells and horns are heard from over the fields— And now I see the beauty and full meaning of that word sound. Nature always possesses a certain sonorousness, as in the hum of insects—the booming of ice—the crowing of cocks in the morning and the barking of dogs in the night—which indicates her sound state. God's voice is but a clear bell sound. I drink in a wonderful health—a cordial—in sound. The effect of the slightest tinkling in the horizon measures my own soundness. I thank God for sound⟦:⟧ it always mounts, and makes me mount.

3 March 1841, Journal *1:276–77*

❦ Cloudy but spring-like. When the frost comes out of the ground there is a corresponding thawing of the man. The earth is now half bare. These march winds which make the woods roar—& fill the world with life & bustle—appear to wake up the trees out of their winter sleep & excite the sap to flow. I have no doubt they serve some such use as well as to hasten the evaporation of the snow & water. . . .

Though cloudy the air excites me. Yesterday all was tight as a stricture on my breast—today all is loosened. It is a different element from what it was. The sides of bushy hills where the snow is melted look through this air as if I were under the influence of some intoxicating liquor— The earth is not quite steady nor palpable to my sense—a little idealized. . . .

I was reminded this morning before I rose of those undescribed ambrosial mornings of summer which I can remember—when a thousand birds were heard gently twittering and ushering in the light—like the argument to a new canto of an epic and heroic poem. The serenity the infinite promise of such a morning! The song or twitter of birds drips from the leaves like dew. Then there was something divine and immortal in our life.

9–10 March 1852, Journal *4:382–84*

❦ When it [is] proposed to me to go abroad, rub off some rust, and *better my condition* in a worldly sense, I fear lest my life will lose some of its homeliness. If these fields and streams and woods, the phenomena of nature here, and the simple occupations of the inhabitants should cease to interest and inspire me, no culture or wealth would atone for the loss. I fear the dissipation that travelling, going into society, even the best, the enjoyment of intellectual luxuries, imply. If Paris is much in your mind, if it is more and more to you, Concord is less and less, and yet it would be a wretched bargain to accept the proudest Paris in exchange for my native village. At best, Paris could only be a school in which to learn to live here, a stepping-stone to Concord, a school in which to fit for this university. I wish so to live ever as to derive my satisfactions and inspirations from the commonest events, every-day phenomena, so that what my senses hourly perceive, my daily walk, the conversation of my neighbors, may inspire me, and I may dream of no heaven but that which lies about me. A man may acquire a taste for wine or brandy, and so lose his love for water, but should we not pity him?

The sight of a marsh hawk in Concord meadows is worth more to me than the entry of the allies into Paris. In this sense I am not ambitious. I do not wish my native soil to become exhausted and run out through neglect. Only that travelling is good which reveals to me the value of home and enables me to enjoy it better. That man is the richest whose pleasures are the cheapest.

11 March 1856, Journal *VIII:204–5*

❧ THERE IS A SORT of homely truth and naturalness in some books, which is very rare to find, and yet looks quite cheap.

There may be nothing lofty in the sentiment—or polished in the expression—but it is careless—countrified talk. The scholar rarely writes as well as the farmer talks. Homeliness is a great merit in a book—it is next to beauty and a high art. Some have this merit only—a few homely expressions redeem

them.— Rusticity is pastoral—but affectation merely civil—
The scholar does not make his most familiar experience come
gracefully to the aid of his expression—and hence, though he
live in it—his books contain no tolerable pictures of the country and simple life. Very few men can speak of nature with any
truth— They confer no favor—they do not speak a good word
for her. Most cry better than they speak— You can get more
nature out of them by pinching them than by addressing them.
It is naturalness, and not simply good nature, that interests. I
like better the surliness with which the wood chopper speaks
of his woods, handling them as indifferently as his axe—than
the mealy mouthed enthusiasm of the lover of nature. Better
that the primrose by the river's brim be a yellow primrose and
nothing more, than the victim of his bouquet or herbarium—to
shine with the flickering dull light of his imagination, and not
the golden gleam of a star.

13 March 1841, Journal *1:286–87*

🍃 A MILD SPRING DAY— I must hie to the [Great] Meadows.
The air is full of blue-birds The ground almost entirely bare.
The villagers are out in the sun—and every man is happy
whose work takes him out doors— I go by [Sleepy] Hollow
toward the Great Fields— I lean over a rail to hear what is in
the air liquid with the blue-bird's warble. My life partakes of
infinity. The air is as deep as our natures. Is the drawing in
of this vital air attended with no more glorious results than
I witness? The air is a velvet cushion against which I press
my ear— I go forth to make new demands on life. I wish to
begin this summer well—to do something in it worthy of it &

of me— To transcend my daily routine—& that of my towns-
men[—]to have my immortality now—that it be in the *quality*
of my daily life. To pay the greatest price—the—greatest tax
of any man in Concord—& enjoy the most! I will give all I am
for *my* nobility. I will pay all my days for *my* success. I pray
that the life of this spring & summer may ever lie fair in my
memory. May I dare as I have never done.— [May] I persevere
as I have never done. May I purify myself anew as with fire &
water—soul & body— May my melody not be wanting to the
season. May I gird myself to be a hunter of the beautiful that
naught escape me— May I attain to a youth never attained[.]
I am eager to report the glory of the universe.— [M]ay I be
worthy to do it— To have got through with regarding human
values so as not to be distracted from regarding divine values.
It is reasonable that a man should be something worthier at the
end of the year than he was at the beginning.

15 March 1852, Journal *4:390*

❦ Aʜ! there is the note of the first flicker, a prolonged, monoto-
nous *wick-wick-wick-wick-wick-wick*, etc., or, if you please, *quick-
quick*, heard far over and through the dry leaves. But how that
single sound peoples and enriches all the woods and fields!
They are no longer the same woods and fields that they were.
This note really *quickens* what was dead. It seems to put a life
into withered grass and leaves and bare twigs, and henceforth
the days shall not be as they have been. It is as when a family,
your neighbors, return to an empty house after a long absence,
and you hear the cheerful hum of voices and the laughter of
children, and see the smoke from the kitchen fire. The doors

are thrown open, and children go screaming through the hall. So the flicker dashes through the aisles of the grove, throws up a window here and cackles out of it, and then there, airing the house. It makes its voice ring up-stairs and down-stairs, and so, as it were, fits it for its habitation and ours, and takes possession. It is as good as a housewarming to all nature. Now I hear and see him louder and nearer on the top of the long-armed white oak, sitting very upright, as is their wont, as it were calling for some of his kind that may also have arrived. . . .

Each new year is a surprise to us. We find that we had virtually forgotten the note of each bird, and when we hear it again it is remembered like a dream, reminding us of a previous state of existence. How happens it that the associations it awakens are always pleasing, never saddening; reminiscences of our sanest hours? The voice of nature is always encouraging.

17–18 March 1858, Journal *X:300–301, 304*

SPRING AGAIN

IT IS A GENIAL and reassuring day; the mere warmth of the west wind amounts almost to balminess. The softness of the air mollifies our own dry and congealed substance. I sit down by a wall to see if I can muse again. We become, as it were, pliant and ductile again to strange but memorable influences; we are led a little way by our genius. We are affected like the earth, and yield to the elemental tenderness; winter breaks up within us; the frost is coming out of me, and I am heaved like the road; accumulated masses of ice and snow dissolve, and thoughts like a freshet pour down unwonted channels. A strain of music comes to solace the traveller over earth's downs and dignify his chagrins, the petty men whom he meets are the shadows of grander to come. Roads lead elsewhither than to Carlisle and Sudbury. The earth is uninhabited but fair to inhabit, like the old Carlisle road. Is then the road so rough that it should be neglected? Not only narrow but rough is the way that leadeth to life everlasting. Our experience does not wear upon us. It is seen to be fabulous or symbolical, and the future is worth expecting. Encouraged, I set out once more to climb the mountain of the earth, for my steps are symbolical steps, and in all my walking I have not reached the top of the earth yet.

21 March 1853, Journal *V:34–35*

A NOTE ON TEXTS

For nearly a century the standard edition has been *The Writings of Henry David Thoreau*, edited by Bradford Torrey and Francis H. Allen, 20 volumes (Boston: Houghton Mifflin, 1906), volumes VII to XX of which comprise the *Journal* (separately numbered I to XIV). The 1906 Houghton Mifflin edition is being superseded by the ongoing *The Writings of Henry D. Thoreau* (Princeton, N.J.: Princeton University Press, 1971–), which among other titles has published seven volumes of the *Journal* to date. The Princeton edition of the *Journal* prints Thoreau's text exactly as it appears in manuscript and retains all peculiarities of his spelling, punctuation, and syntax. The Spirit of Thoreau series makes occasional editorial interpolations—indicated by square brackets—for cases in which the Princeton literal transcription might cause confusion and to provide context for certain passages. Arabic numerals indicate the seven volumes of the Princeton edition; roman numerals, the volumes of the 1906 *Journal* not yet superseded by Princeton.

FURTHER READING

Works by Thoreau

❦ *The Correspondence of Henry David Thoreau.* Edited by Walter Harding and Carl Bode. New York: New York University Press, 1958. Reprint, Westport, Conn.: Greenwood, 1974.

❦ *Early Essays and Miscellanies.* Edited by Joesph J. Moldenhauer and Edwin Moser, with Alexander Kern. Princeton: Princeton University Press, 1975.

❦ *Excursions.* Boston: Houghton Mifflin, 1863.

❦ *Faith in a Seed: The Dispersion of Seeds and Other Late Natural History Writings.* Edited by Bradley P. Dean. Washington, D.C.: Island Press, 1993.

❦ *The Journal of Henry David Thoreau.* Volumes I–XIV. Edited by Bradford Torrey and Francis Allen. 1906. Reprint, Boston: Houghton Mifflin, 1949.

❦ *Journal.* Volumes 1–6, 8. Elizabeth Hall Witherell, editor-in-chief. Princeton: Princeton University Press, 1981–2002.

❦ *The Natural History Essays.* Edited by Robert Sattelmeyer. Salt Lake City: Peregrine Smith, 1980.

❦ *Reform Papers.* Edited by Wendell Glick. Princeton: Princeton University Press, 1973.

❦ *Thoreau's Rediscovered Last Manuscript: Wild Fruits.* Edited by Bradley P. Dean. New York: W. W. Norton, 1999.

❦ *Walden.* Edited by J. Lyndon Shanley. Princeton: Princeton University Press, 1971.

❦ *A Week on the Concord and Merrimack Rivers.* Edited by Carl F. Hovde, William Howarth, and Elizabeth Hall Witherell. Princeton: Princeton University Press, 1980.

Further Reading

Selected Editions of Thoreau's Writings on the Seasons

Editors of Thoreau have traditionally respected the associations he routinely drew between himself and the seasons. "The seasons and all their changes are in me," he wrote in his journal on 26 October 1857, and H. G. O. Blake, who along with Emerson was among Thoreau's first editors, prepared an edition of journal writings in four volumes and arranged them in a seasonal motif under these titles:

🌱 *Early Spring in Massachusetts.* Boston: Houghton Mifflin, 1881.
🌱 *Summer: From the Journal of Henry D. Thoreau.* Boston: Houghton Mifflin, 1884.
🌱 *Winter: From the Journal of Henry D. Thoreau.* Boston: Houghton Mifflin, 1888.
🌱 *Autumn: From the Journal of Henry D. Thoreau.* Boston: Houghton Mifflin, 1892.

Numerous one-volume selected editions of Thoreau's writings have continued to represent his response to seasonal influences in various ways. Following are several recent examples:

🌱 *Henry David Thoreau: An American Landscape.* Edited and illustrated by Robert L. Rothwell. New York: Marlowe, 1991.
🌱 *Henry David Thoreau: Sweet Wild World.* Selections from the journals arranged as poetry by William M. White. Boston: Charles River Books, 1982.
🌱 *Selections from the Journals of Henry David Thoreau: In the Woods and Fields of Concord.* Edited by Walter Harding. Salt Lake City: Gibbs M. Smith, 1982.
🌱 *Thoreau's World: Miniatures from His Journal.* Edited by Charles R. Anderson. Englewood Cliffs, N.J.: Prentice-Hall, 1971.
🌱 *Wood-Notes Wild: Walking with Thoreau.* Selections arranged as poetry by Mary Kullberg, with drawings by Christine Stetter. Carbondale: Southern Illinois University Press, 1995.

Further Reading

Other Works Cited and Secondary Sources

❧ Buell, Lawrence. *The Environmental Imagination: Thoreau, Nature Writing, and the Formation of American Culture.* Cambridge: Harvard University Press, 1995.

❧ *The Cambridge Companion to Henry David Thoreau.* Edited by Joel Myerson. Cambridge: Cambridge University Press, 1995. In this volume, see particularly Lawrence Buell, "Thoreau and the Natural Environment"; Ronald Wesley Hoag, "Thoreau's Later Natural History Writings"; Leonard J. Neufeldt, "Thoreau in His Journal"; and Robert D. Richardson Jr., "Thoreau and Concord."

❧ Cameron, Sharon. *Writing Nature: Henry Thoreau's* Journal. New York and Oxford: Oxford University Press, 1985.

❧ Emerson, Ralph Waldo. *The Collected Works of Ralph Waldo Emerson.* Edited by Alfred R.Ferguson, Joseph Slater et al. 5 volumes to date. Cambridge: Harvard University Press, 1971–. Cited in the Introduction as *CW.*

❧ ———. *The Complete Sermons of Ralph Waldo Emerson.* Edited by Albert J. von Frank et al. 4 volumes. Columbia: University of Missouri Press, 1989–92. Cited in the Introduction as *CS.*

❧ ———. *The Journals and Miscellaneous Notebooks of Ralph Waldo Emerson.* Edited by William H. Gilman, Ralph H. Orth et al. 16 volumes. Cambridge: Harvard University Press, 1960–82. Cited in the Introduction as *JMN.*

❧ Foster, David R. *Thoreau's Country: Journey through a Transformed Landscape.* Cambridge: Harvard University Press, 1999.

❧ Harding, Walter. *The Days of Henry Thoreau: A Biography.* Princeton: Princeton University Press, 1992.

❧ Lebeaux, Richard. *Thoreau's Seasons.* Amherst: University of Massachusetts Press, 1984.

❧ Mitchell, John Hanson. *Walking towards Walden: A Pilgrimage in Search of Place.* Reading, Mass.: Addison-Wesley, 1995.

❧ Richardson, Robert D., Jr. *Henry Thoreau: A Life of the Mind.* Berkeley and Los Angeles: University of California Press, 1986.

THE SPIRIT OF THOREAU

"How many a man has dated a new era in his life from the reading of a book," wrote Henry David Thoreau in *Walden*. Today that book, perhaps more than any other American work, continues to provoke, inspire, and change lives all over the world, and each rereading is fresh and challenging. Yet as Thoreau's countless admirers know, there is more to the man than *Walden*. An engineer, poet, teacher, naturalist, lecturer, and political activist, he truly had several more lives to lead, and each one speaks forcefully to us today.

The Spirit of Thoreau introduces the thoughts of a great writer on a variety of important topics, some that we readily associate him with, some that may be surprising. Each book includes selections from his familiar published works as well as from less well known and recently discovered lectures, letters, and journal entries. Thoreau claimed that "to read well, that is, to read true books in a true spirit, is a noble exercise, and one that will task the reader more than any exercise which the customs of the day esteem." The volume editors and the Thoreau Society believe that you will find these new aspects of Thoreau an exciting "exercise" indeed.

The Thoreau Society is honored to bring you these titles in cooperation with the University of Massachusetts Press. The publisher of many important studies of Thoreau and other Transcendentalists, the press is also widely recognized for its outstanding titles on several aspects of New England culture.

You are invited to continue exploring Thoreau by joining our society. For more than sixty years we have presented publications, annual gatherings, and other programs to further the appreciation of

The Spirit of Thoreau

Thoreau's thought and writings. In ways that the author of *Walden* could not have imagined, his message is still changing lives in a brand-new era.

For membership information, write to The Thoreau Society, 55 Old Bedford Road, Concord, Massachusetts 01742; call 978-369-5310; or visit our website www.thoreausociety.org.

WESLEY T. MOTT
Series Editor
The Thoreau Society

❦

RONALD A. BOSCO,
Distinguished University Professor of English and American
Literature at the University at Albany, State University of
New York, is past-president of The Thoreau Society.

❦

ROBERT D. RICHARDSON JR
is the author of *Henry Thoreau: A Life of the Mind* and
Emerson: The Mind on Fire.